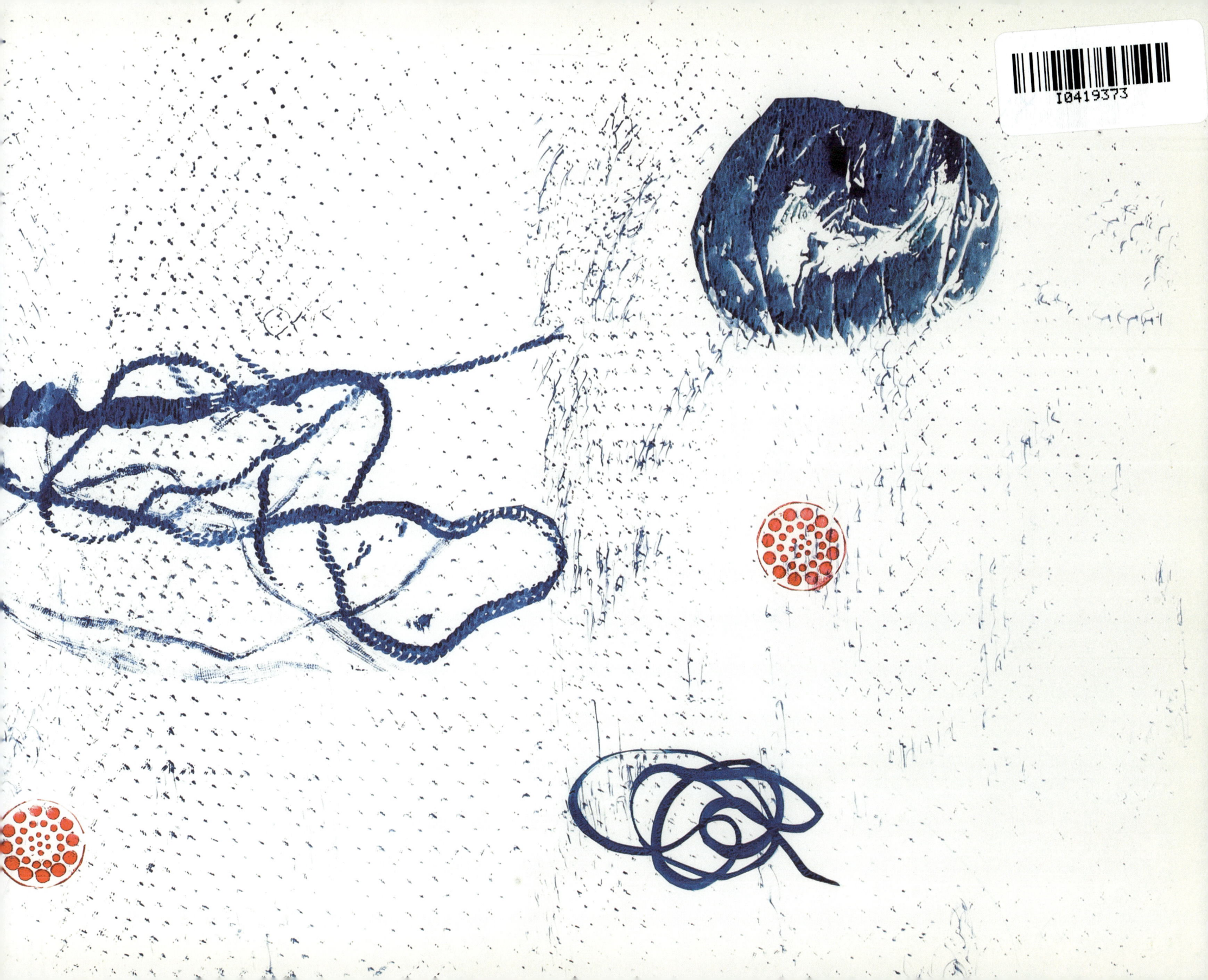

BASTIENNE SCHMIDT   topography of quiet

BASTIENNE SCHMIDT

topography of quiet

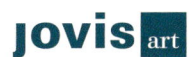

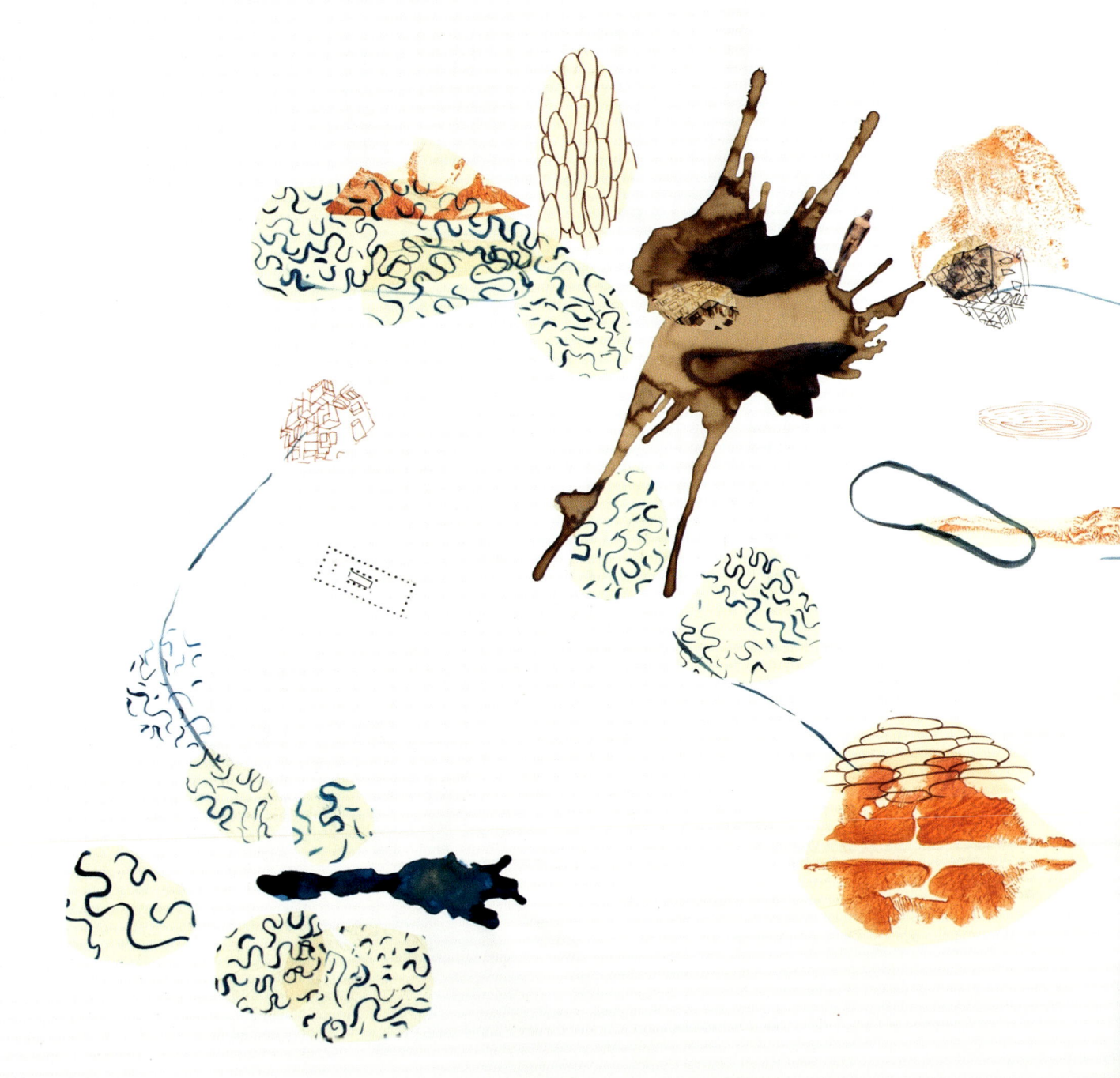

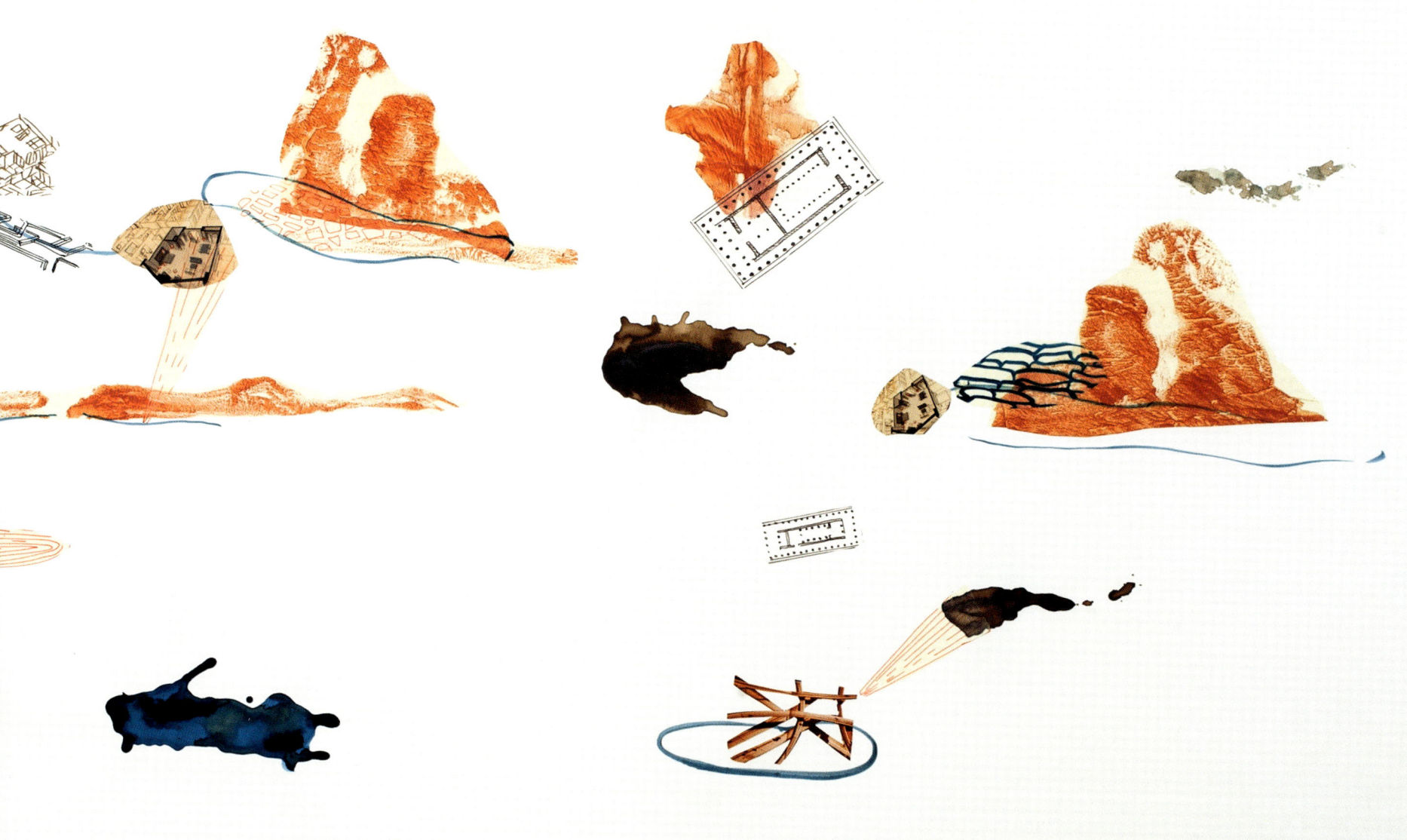

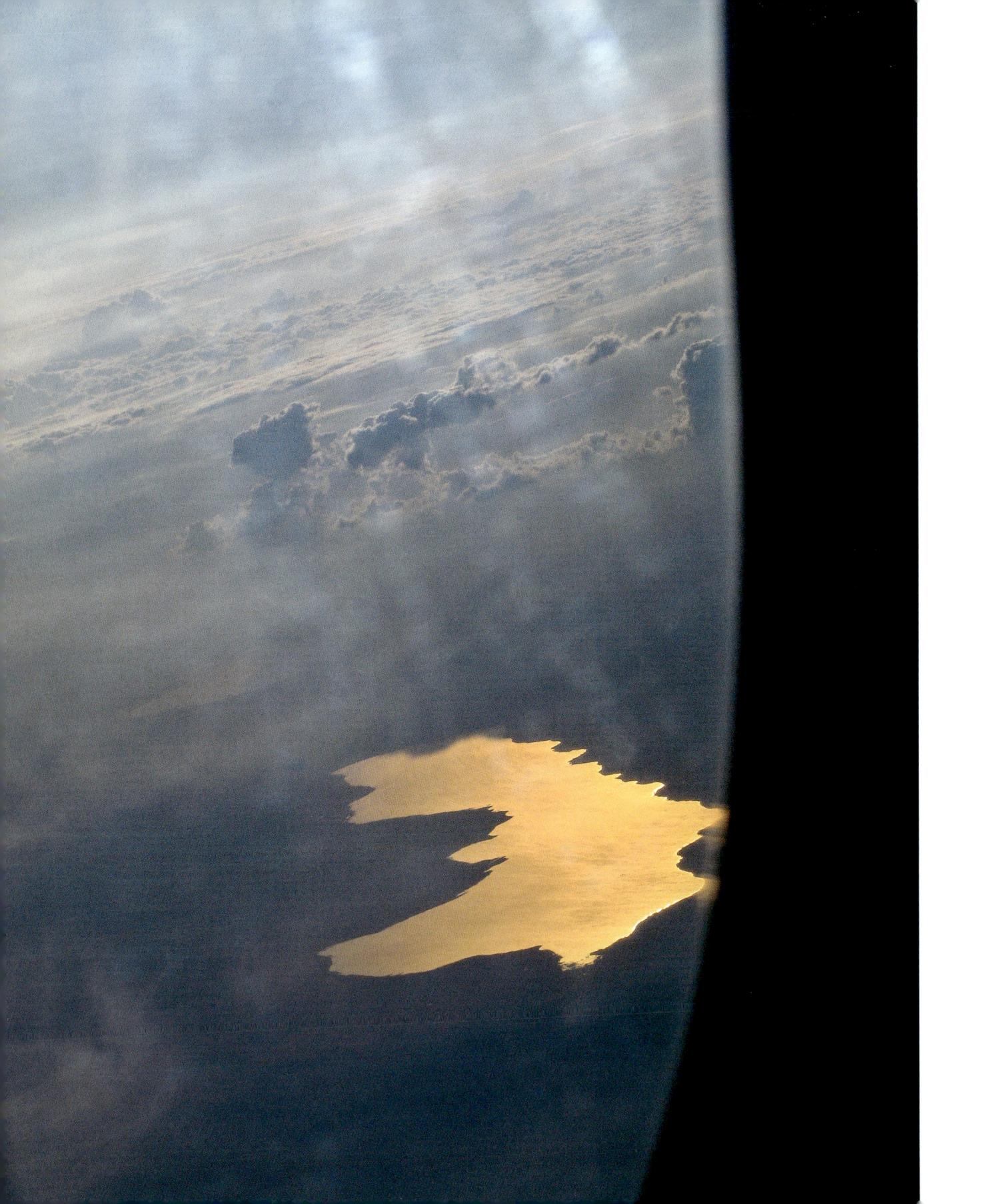

topography [tǝ'pägrǝfē]

noun

the arrangement of the natural and artificial physical features of an area, a detailed description or representation on a map of such features.
Topography is the study of Earth's surface shape and features or those of planets, moons, and asteroids. The term topography originated in ancient Greece and continued in ancient Rome, as the detailed description of a place. The word comes from the Greek words τόπος (topos, place) and γραφία (graphia, writing). In Classical Literature this refers to writing about a place or places.

quiet ['kwīǝt]

adjective

(quieter, quietest)
making little or no noise
without being disturbed or interrupted

On Memories, Maps, Stains, and Others

Nessia Pope in Conversation
with Bastienne Schmidt

NP This is our second interview together. I am honored to be involved in your new book and very pleased to see that your work has come full circle. Is that the idea of this book—the confirmation of a journey?

BS Thanks for continuing our dialogue. Yes, this book is about journeys. Traveling and being exposed to different parts of the world influenced me as an artist early on. As a child, our parents would pack the five kids in our old Ford Taunus and drive 1,000 miles from Greece to Germany, crossing into Yugoslavia, Italy, and Austria. These summer trips were incredibly inspiring. We were the moving part wrapped tightly like a cocoon; passing through changing landscapes; seeing the difference in the physical structures of houses and storefronts; watching people working in the fields. In my mind, I compared all of these small visible systems of life. I think that's where I get my love of typologies, topographies, and maps.

NP Seems like such a happy childhood! Although the landscapes and cultures are wildly distinct from one another, you are attracted by forms and patterns that have a common denominator: large scale earth formations, the undulations of nature, weaving lines, the meticulous arrangements of knotted cords, and taut looms.

BS It was an idyllic childhood in the sense that there was a lot of freedom and space to wander. I was pretty much a daydreamer. Forms and patterns always interested me, from the smallest organism observed under a microscope to the massive landscape seen from an airplane.

NP The idea of macrocosm and microcosm is always present in your work—what you see from above and what you see from below. I remember you telling me that this is a process that is understood better with age …

BS When I was in my teens and twenties, there was always the urge to go out into the world, to explore and discover. The older I get, the more I realize that these principles are very similar. In my photo-graphs and drawings, I like to change the perspective and viewpoint. Reorganizing the plane of perception feels very freeing to me.

NP In your works on paper, you utilize coffee, ink, polymer paint, lint, soap—all humble materials. Your drawings are very delicate, like Chinese landscapes, yet they have rich textures and carry much information; they seem to reflect the complexity of the world. Is that what you have in mind? The patterned layers overlap and float on the page. How do you achieve this result?

BS I am in part inspired by the long format of Japanese and Chinese scroll drawings, in terms of delicacy and complexity. As an underpinning to the drawings I often utilize thumbprints or man-made patterns on layers of transparent paper. At times, I only draw mountains and lakes. They become structures, made by mixing coffee with inks, polymer paints, and embedded strings, which I will later use as elements in my drawings. I experiment with materials, and especially enjoy exploring the absorptive capacity of paper. I am obsessed with stains.

NP I know you like stains! People normally hate stains. From a domestic point of view, they are there to be removed. How appropriate you make landscapes that look like stains.

BS When you pour liquid on a page there is an element of being in control and not in control. There is the moment of excitement of the action and the fear of "messing up." The stain that occurs is just an expansion of space. I enjoy the series *Stains* by Ed Ruscha very much—the cataloging of stains. Every stain has a history and a process.

NP Do you think of process—your process—as the work of a woman in the kitchen? Your photographic production has very deep feminist connotations. But I also see a strong connection with Arte Povera artists.

BS I definitely take a lot of cues from domestic materials, like a reinterpretation of a feminist model. Arte Povera used stronger materials, such as stone, metal, and coal, while I use ephemeral materials:

fabric, paper, soaps, and coffee. I like the idea of poor and recycled materials. There was a wall drawing of Sol Lewitt at my college in Italy; the humble materials on a found surface left a deep impression on me.

NP The notion of space plays an important role, principally in your photographs. Many times the object looks simplified with space taking over. I love the volumes that result from this combination of "weights."

BS Space is a concept of the mind. I have no concern to make the space real, because I know that is a construction of an idea where I am faced with innumerous possibilities. A piece of paper is a space. To see something up close is a different idea of space than being far away.

NP There is no such thing as one big center!

BS True, in my drawings and paintings there is no center.

NP What do you usually do when you travel? Do you draw or edit the photographs or do you wait until you are back at the studio?

BS When I am on a trip I am taking everything in. Seeing, touching, smelling, and feeling are usually very intense. It takes me a while to digest what I have experienced. I like to mix the images—a photograph from Burma can be read in context to one from Egypt. I rarely draw on a trip, I am collecting ideas and my camera is my sketchbook.

NP I have a feeling that you are a very bad tourist in the classic sense of the word.

BS That's funny, but totally true. Even if I have a guide I am always running off on my own. I need the sense of quiet to be able to think, and walk, and explore.

NP You utilize architectural details or footprints of buildings like temples to develop the idea of identity and place, which is essential in your work. You define country borders and maps, inventing them as the work develops. The universe is redrawn as you see fit—a conceptual journey I would say.

BS I am creating mind maps that carry visual memories from places that I have been to. Traces and footprints left on the physical ground are reminders of the intangible force of nature and the randomness of borders created by mankind. In contrast, nature draws borders very clearly—mountains or oceans divide places. I am interested in these spaces in between.

NP You pair the works in a very lyrical, poetic way. They complement each other. What directs your choices?

BS The process of pairing images is a combination of structure and playfulness. It's a journey where one image will lead me to the next, a movie without words, a wandering inside the mind. I change the sequence often during the process to open myself to other possibilities. Each time you change the position of an image you tell a different story.

NP This is your fifth book. Does making books inform your work? Do you think about the next publication when you are developing a body of work?

BS Somehow, it always does inform my work—a cross-feeding of form and content. I love making books, so whenever I work on a long-term project, the thought of a book is on my mind. I learned years ago from the photographer Ralph Gibson—who is a master when it comes to conceptualizing his work in books—that you have to take ownership of your work.

In terms of photographic images, on one hand, I draw from my archive, and on the other I create images that belong to a particular narrative. There is a lot of structure and play at work. My previous book *Home Stills* was about a fictional "housewife," a lone figure who ventured out into different landscapes. With *Topography of Quiet*, there is no longer a figure to be seen—it's all about being in space.

New York, May 2013

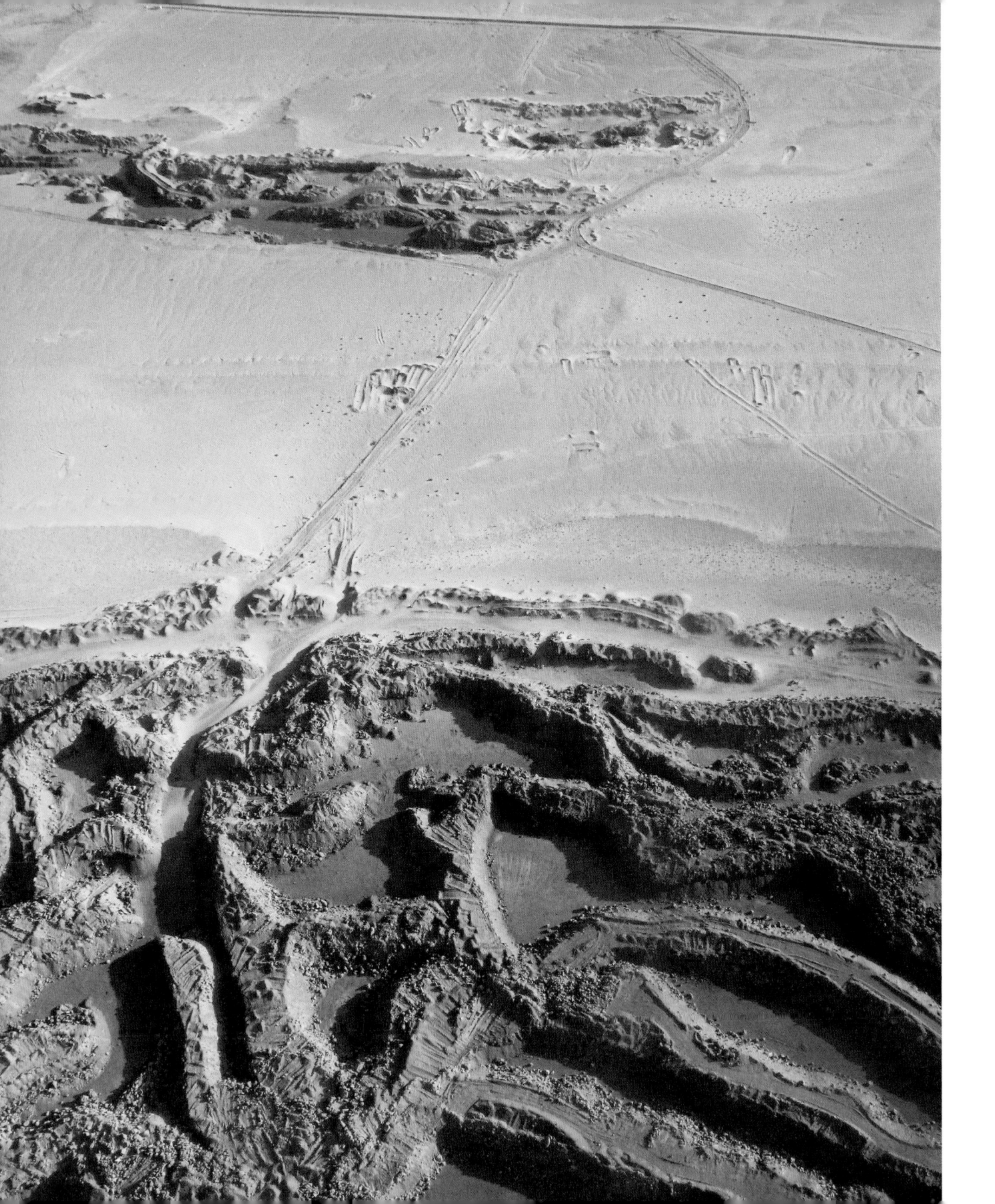

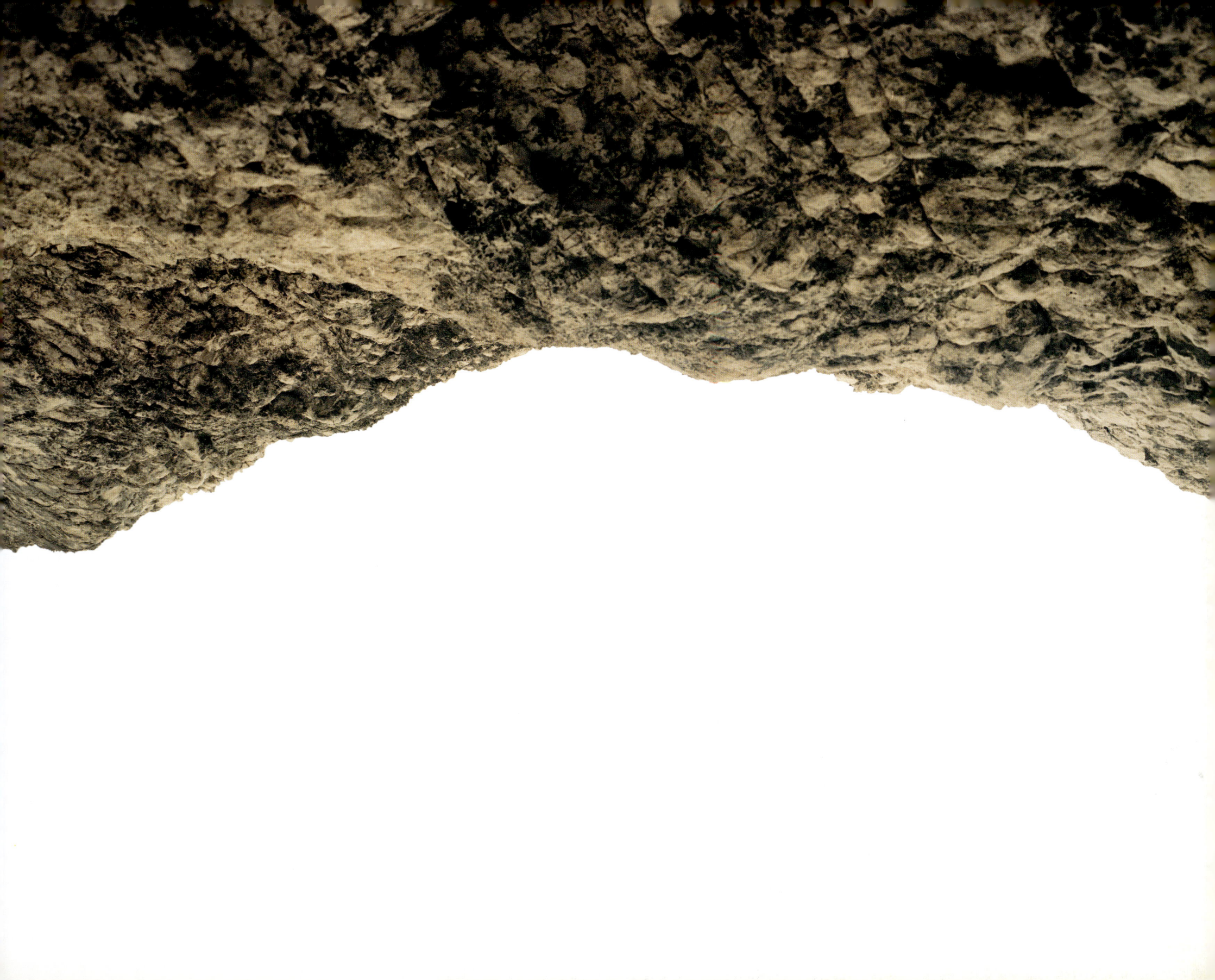

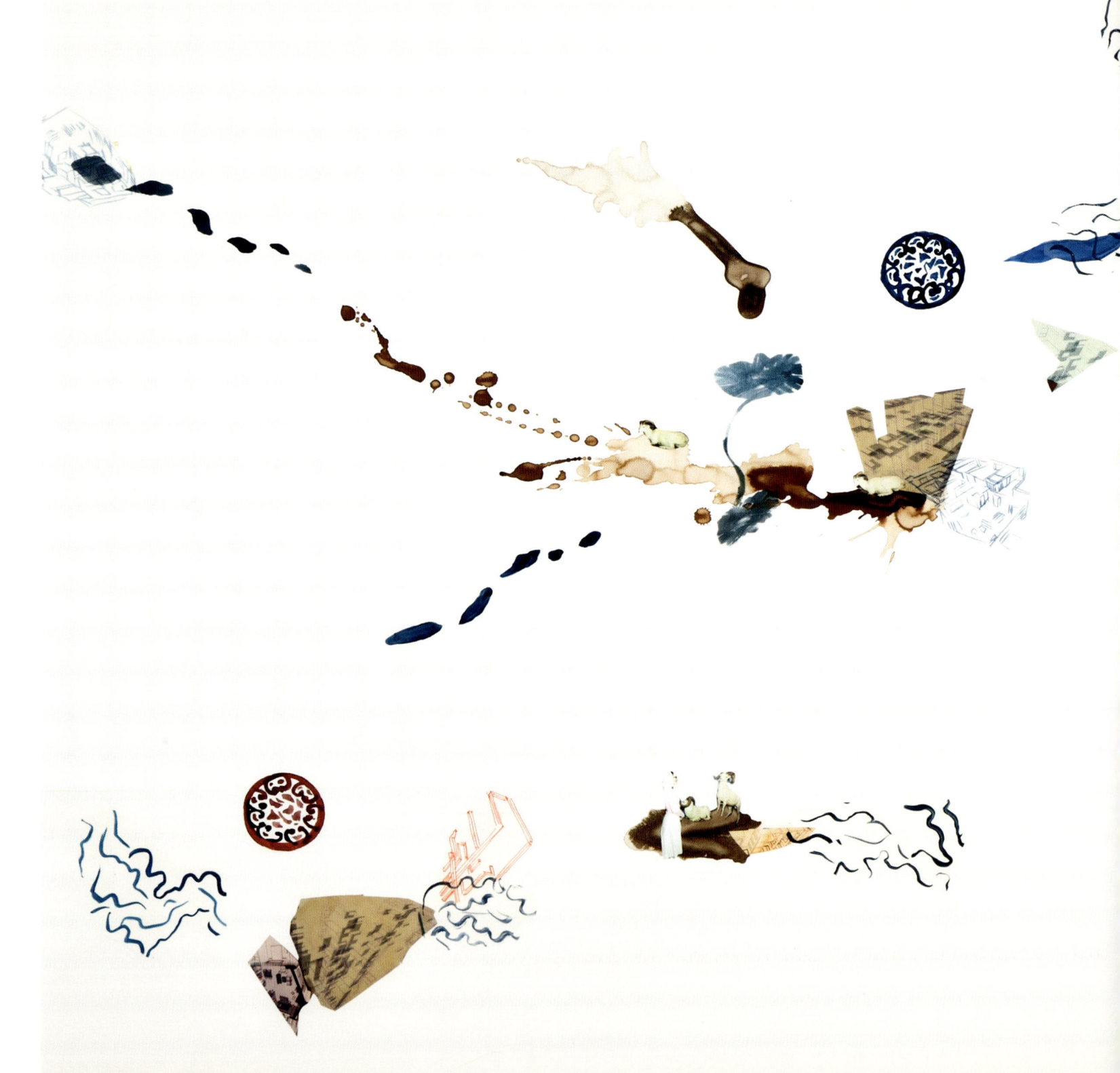

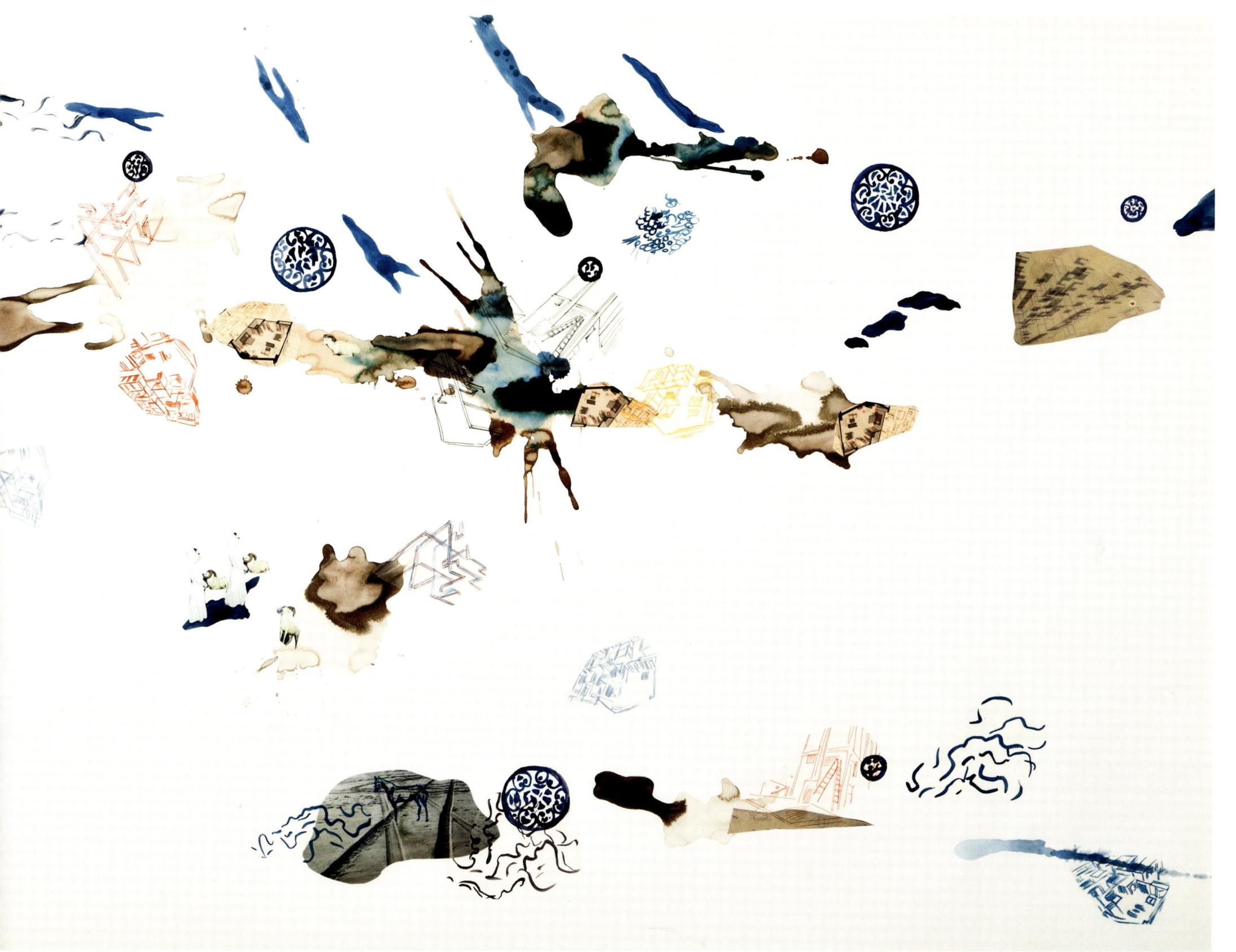

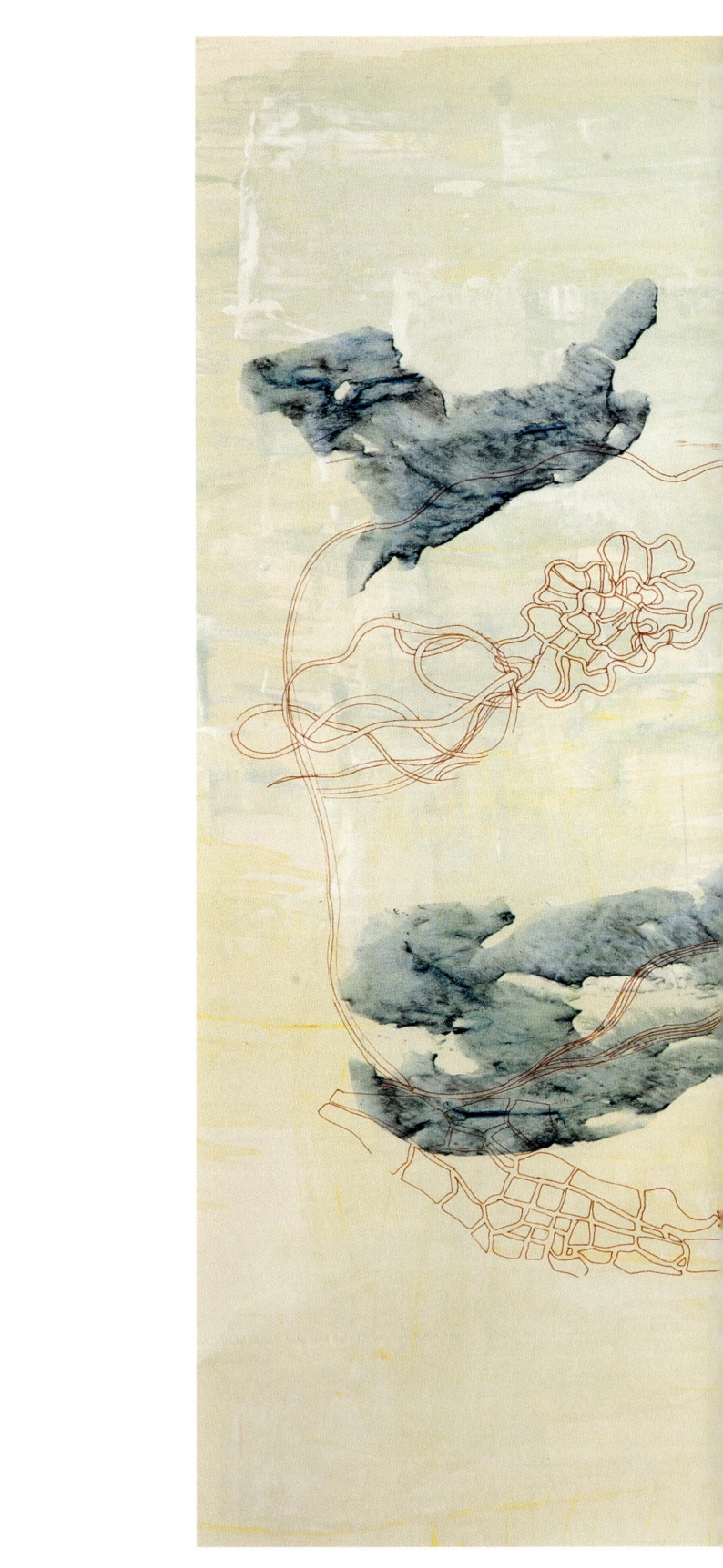

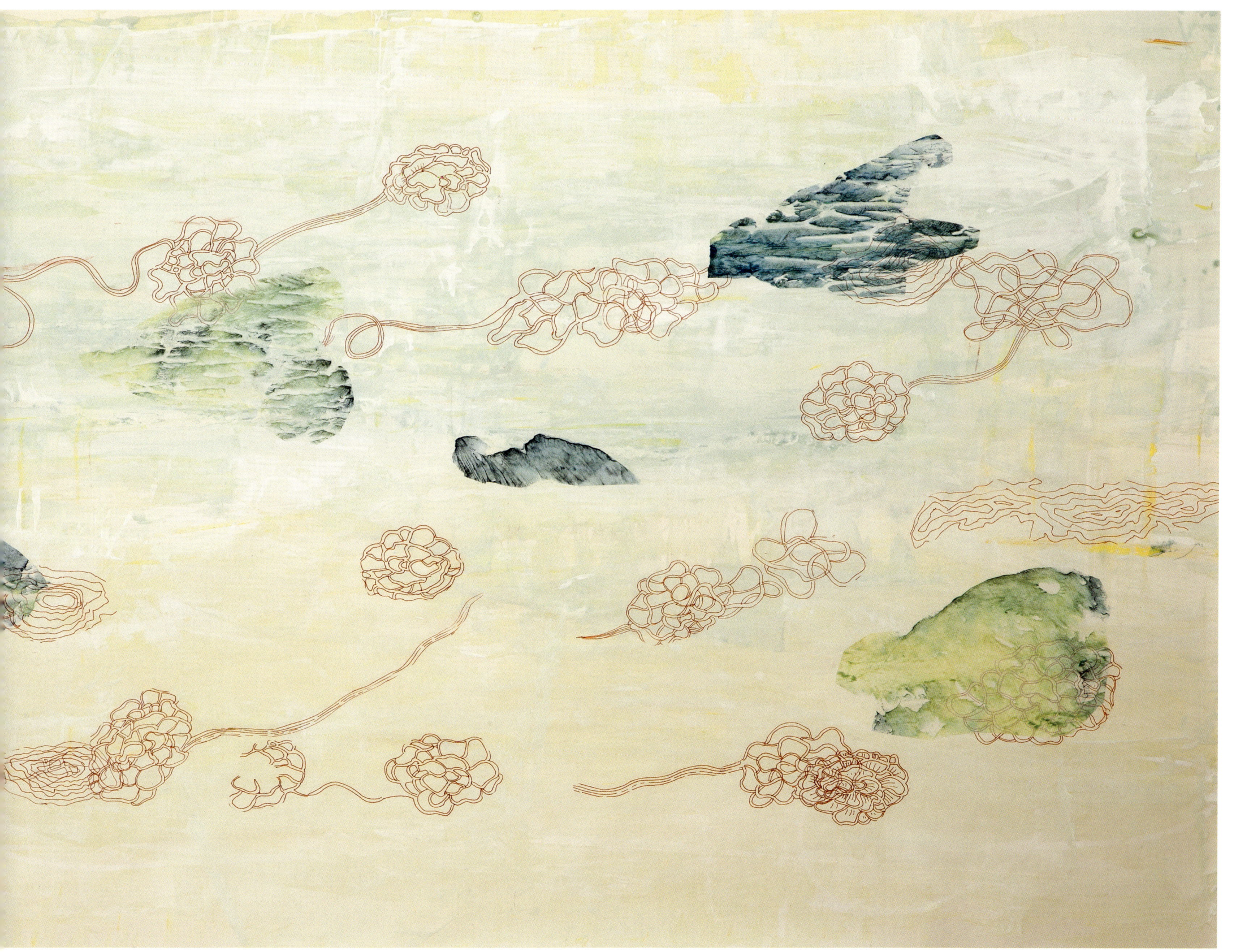

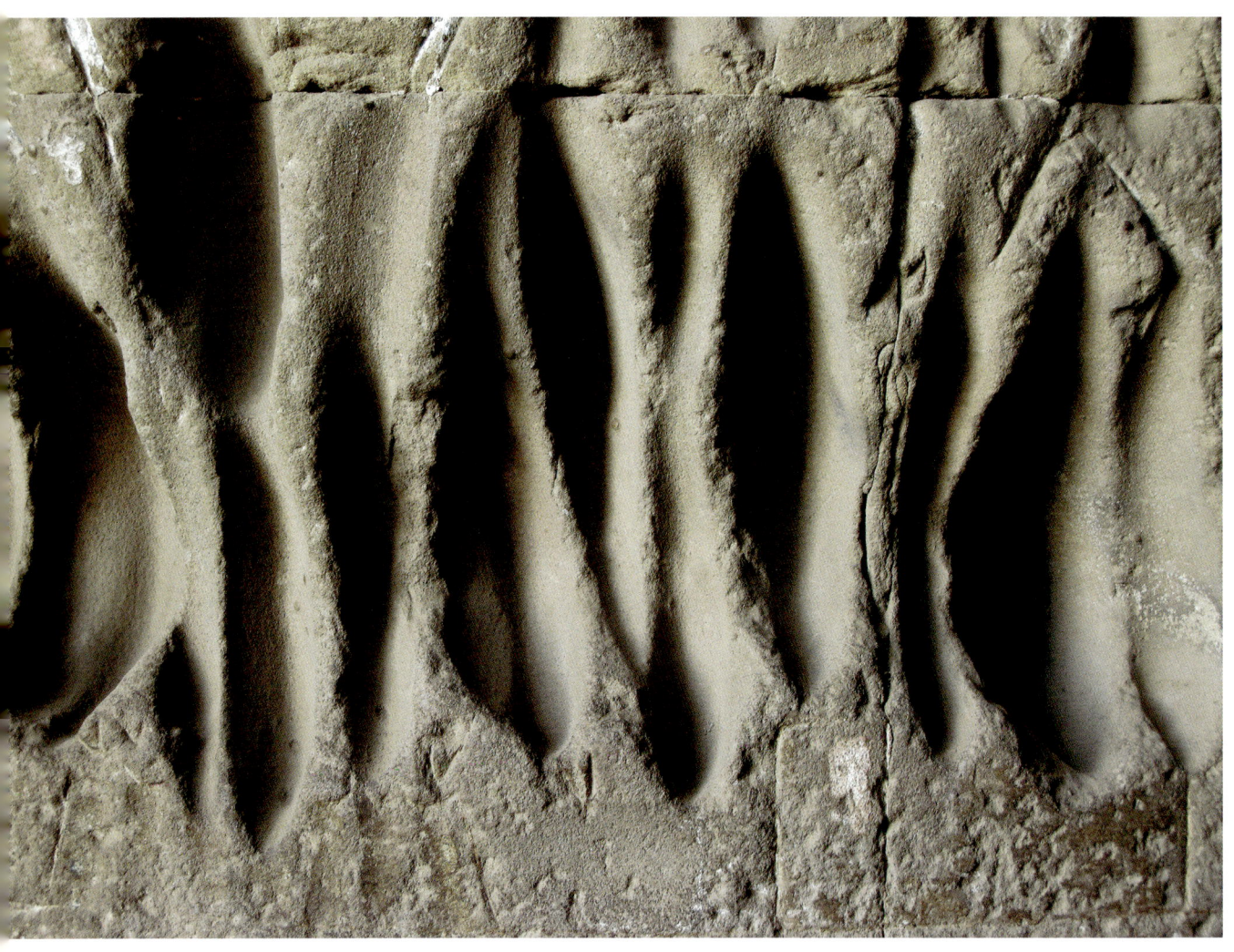

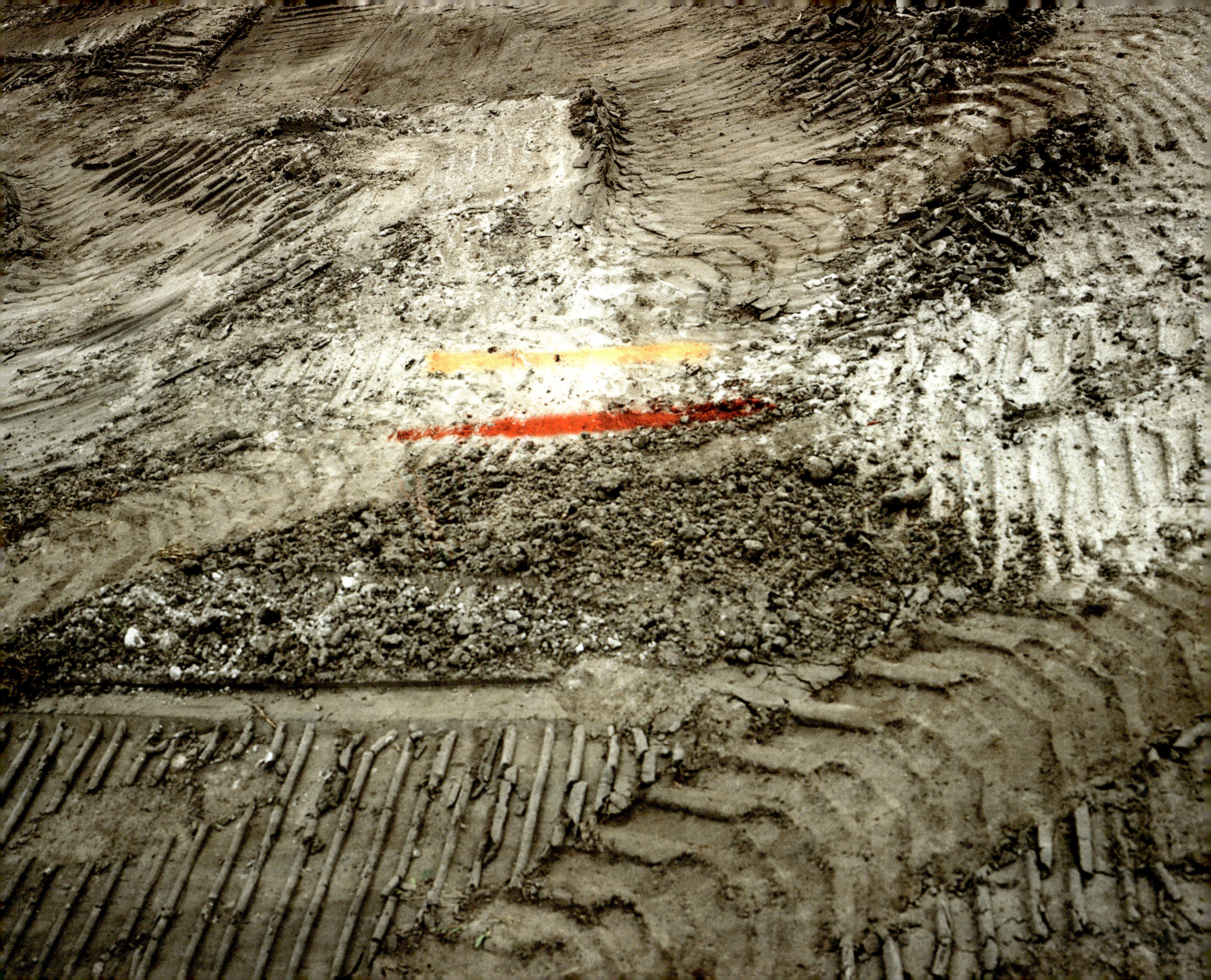

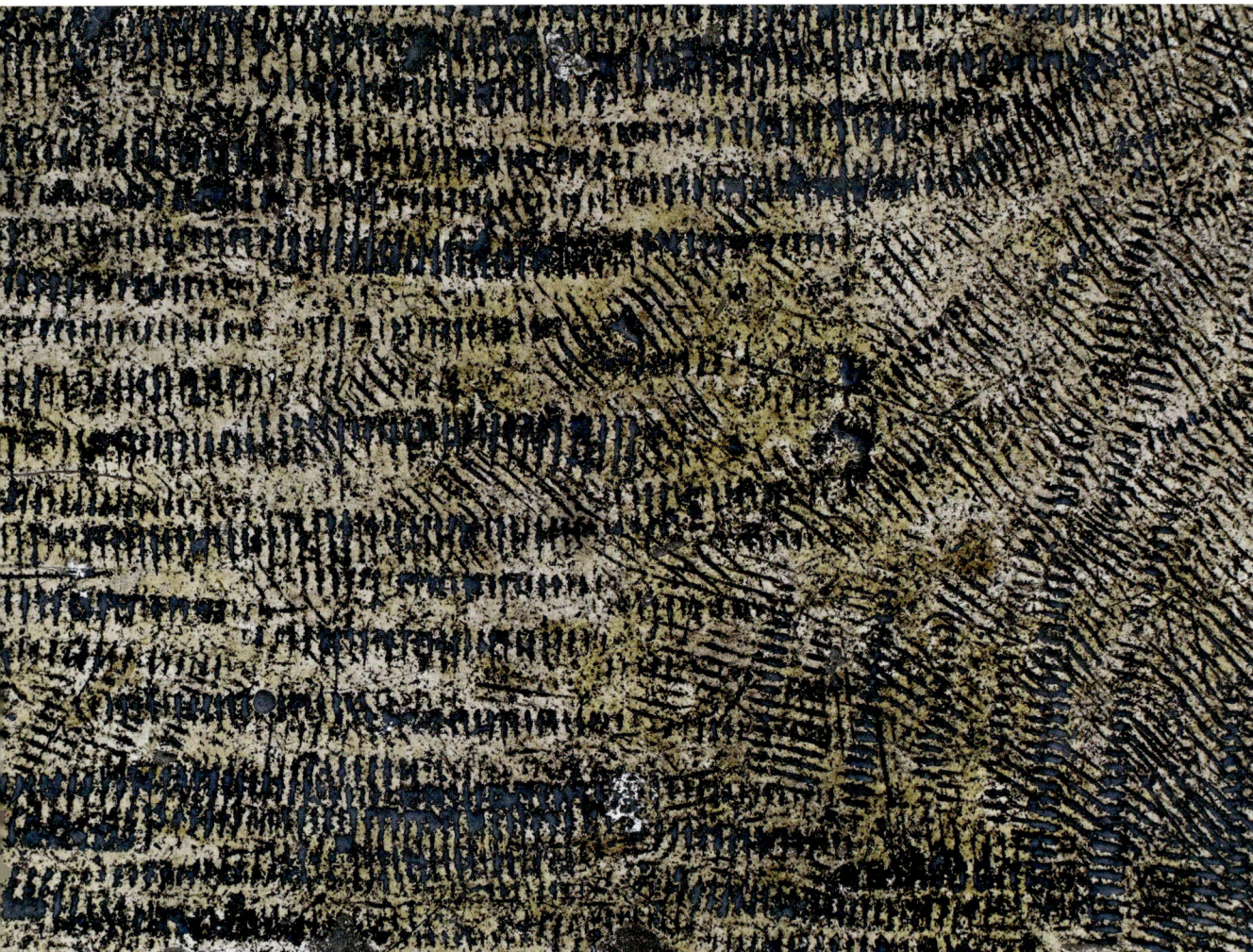

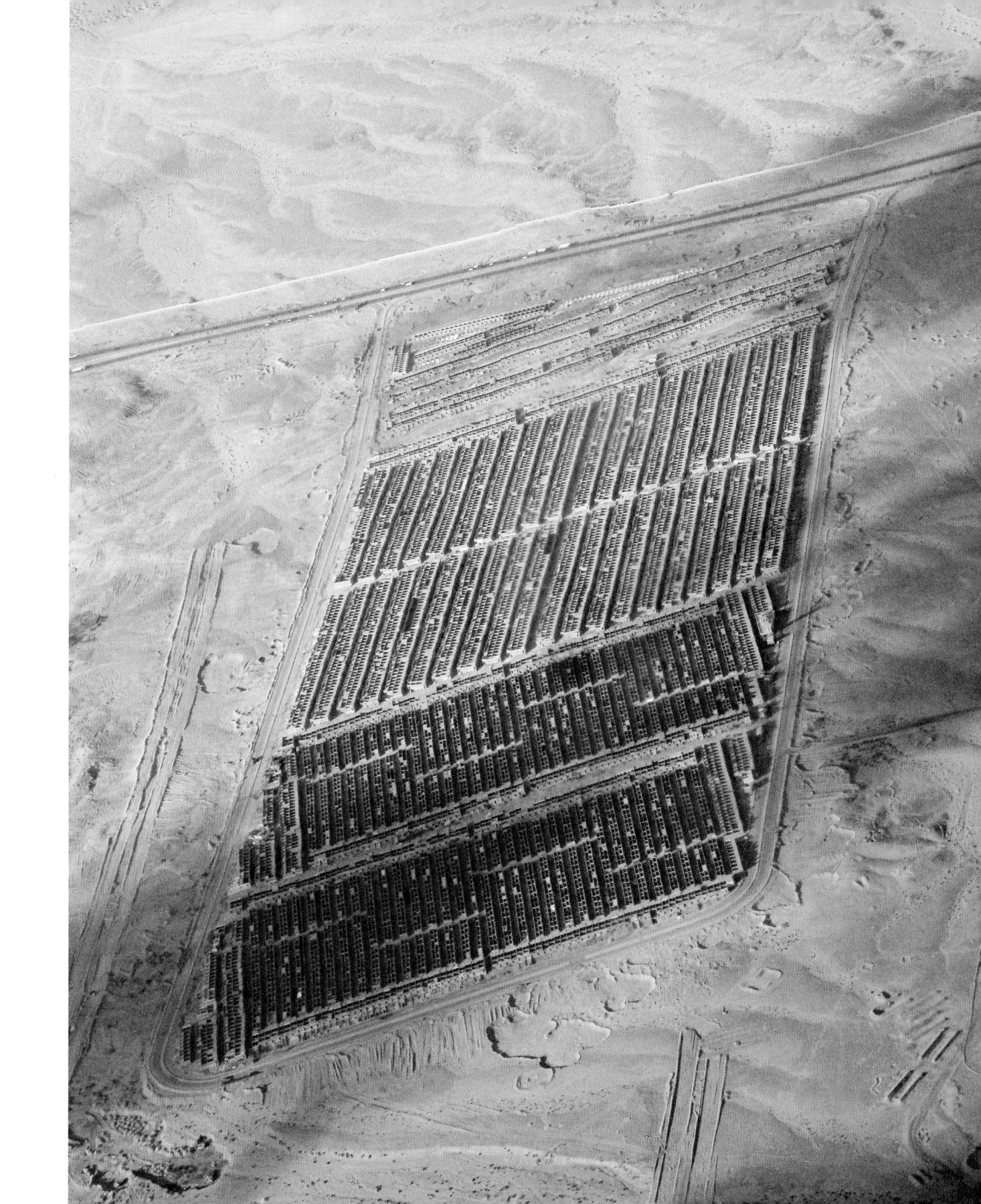

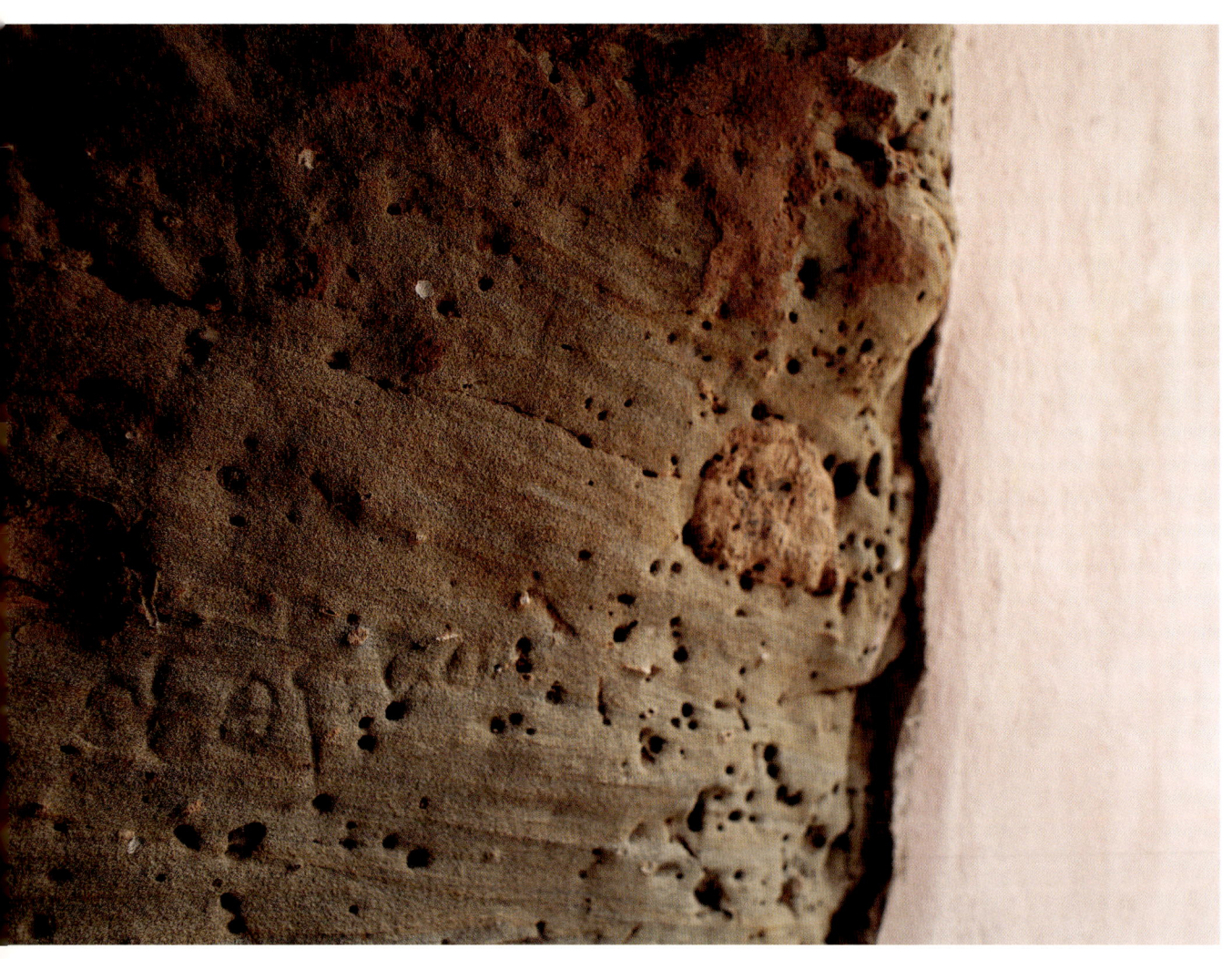

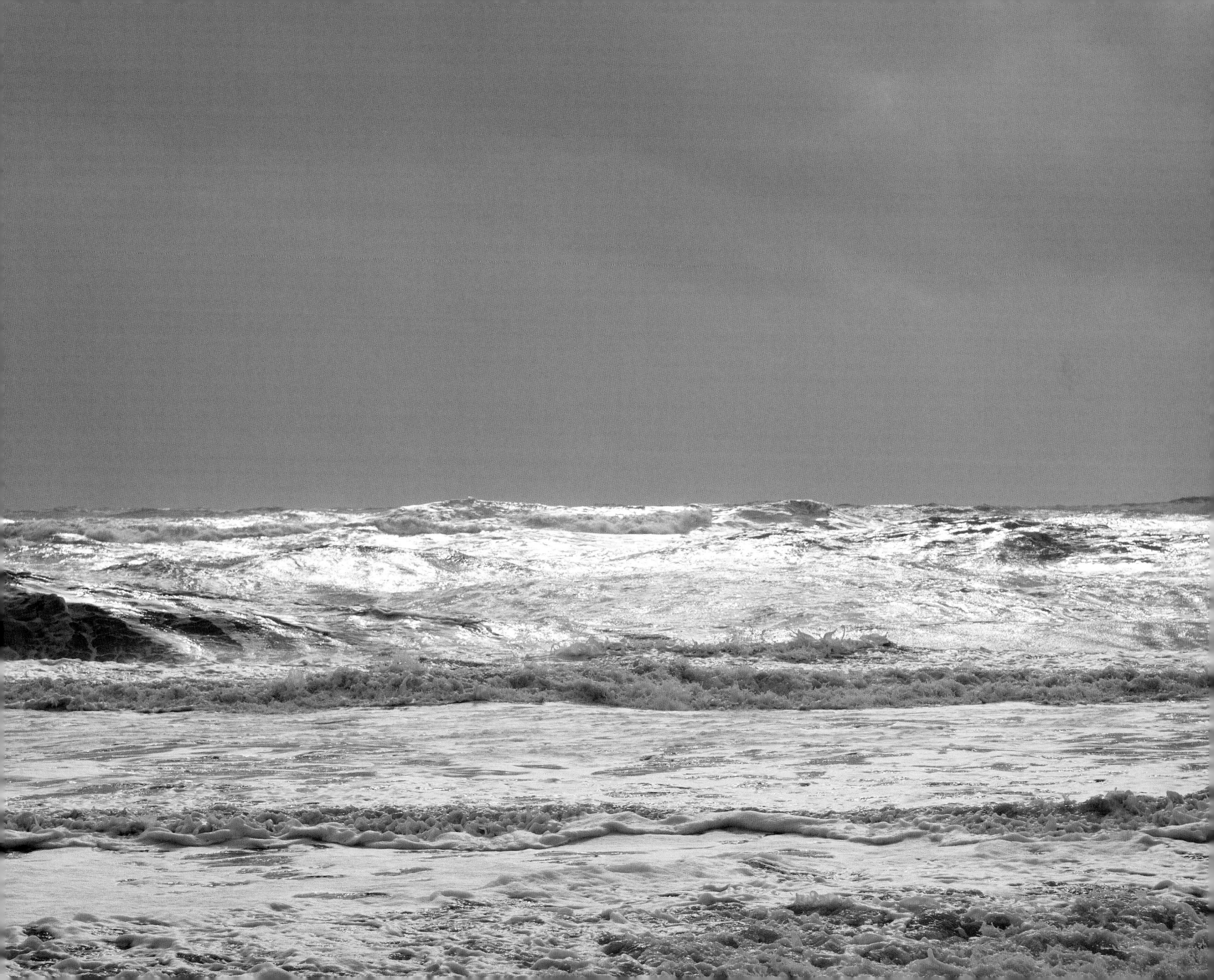

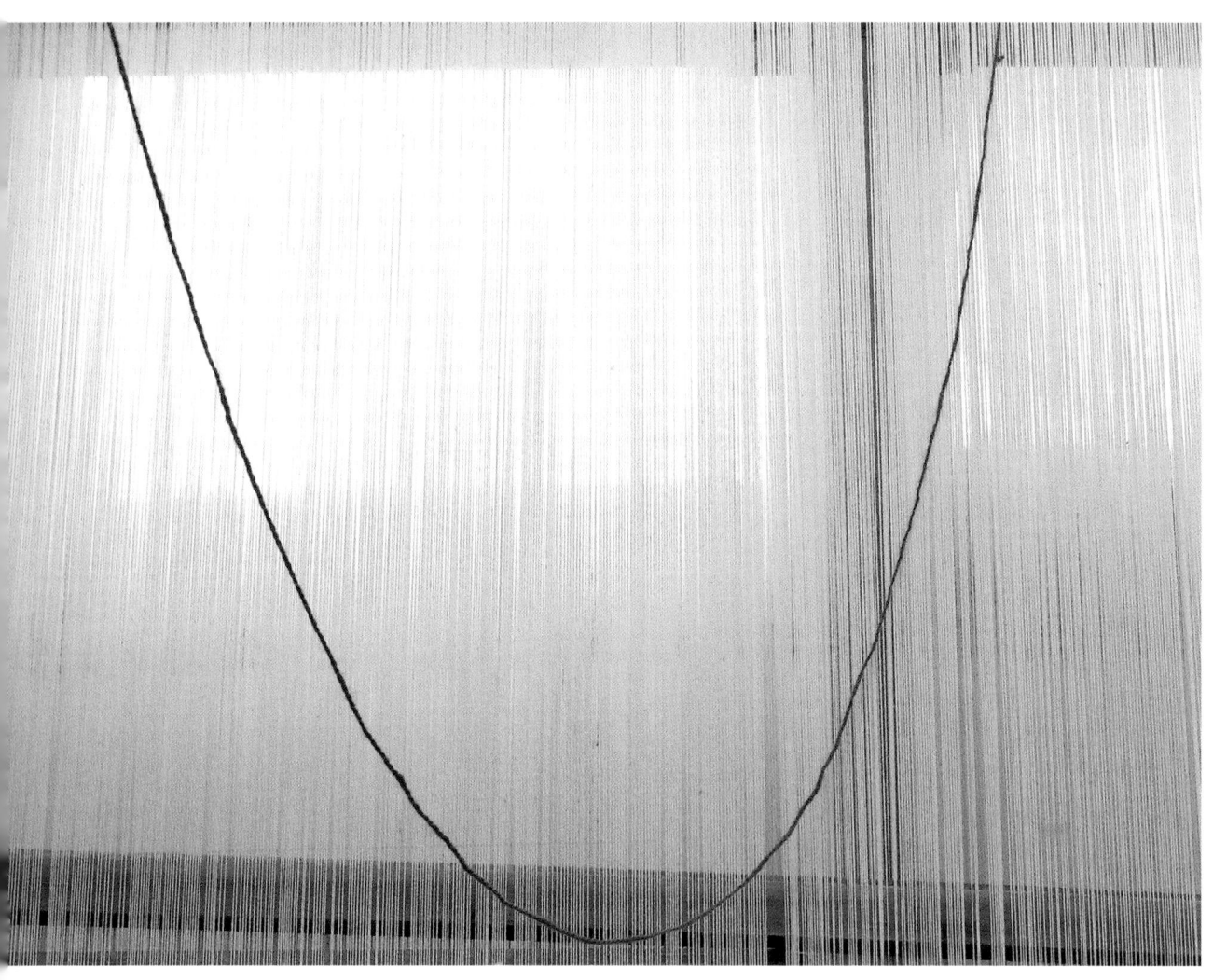

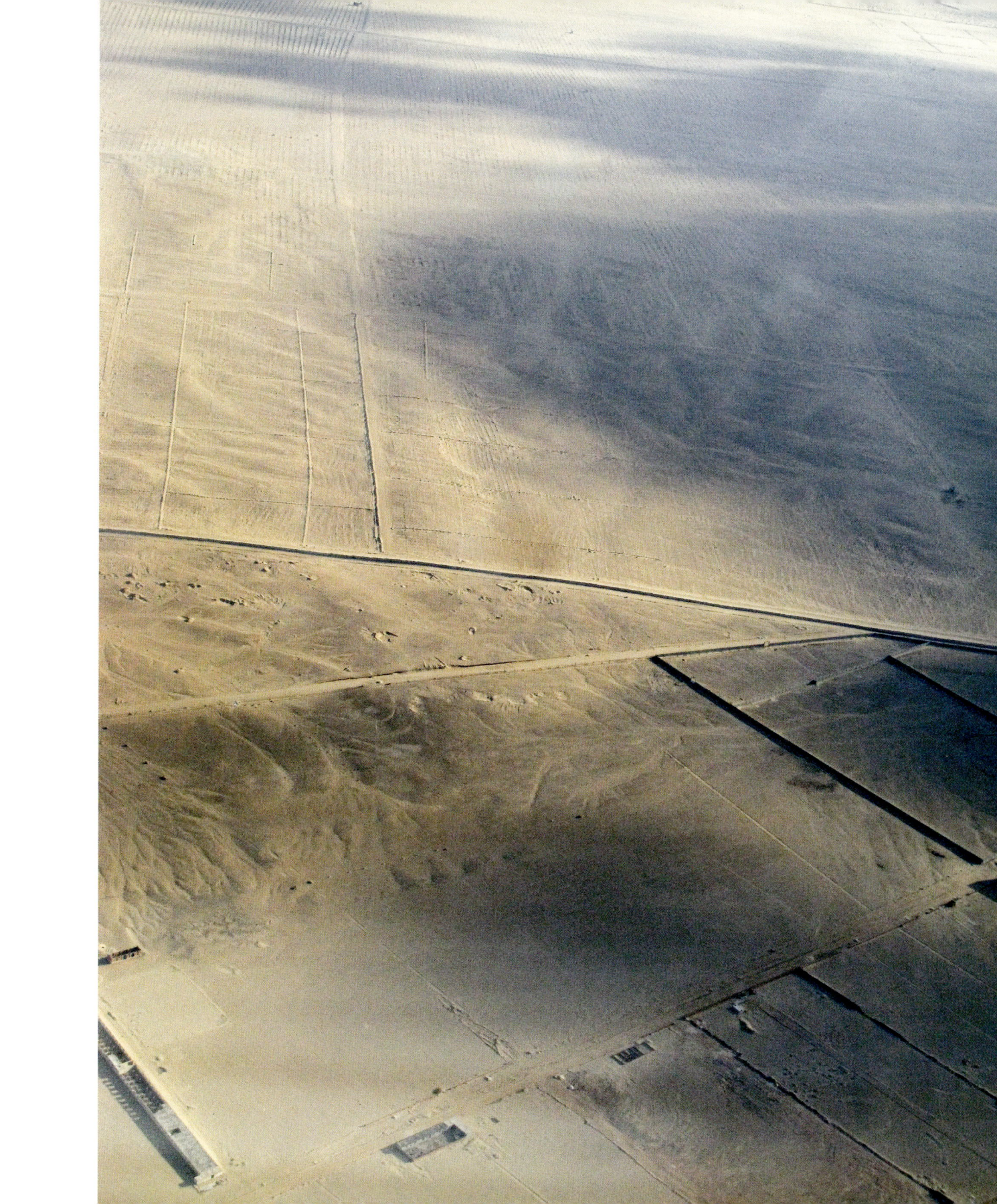

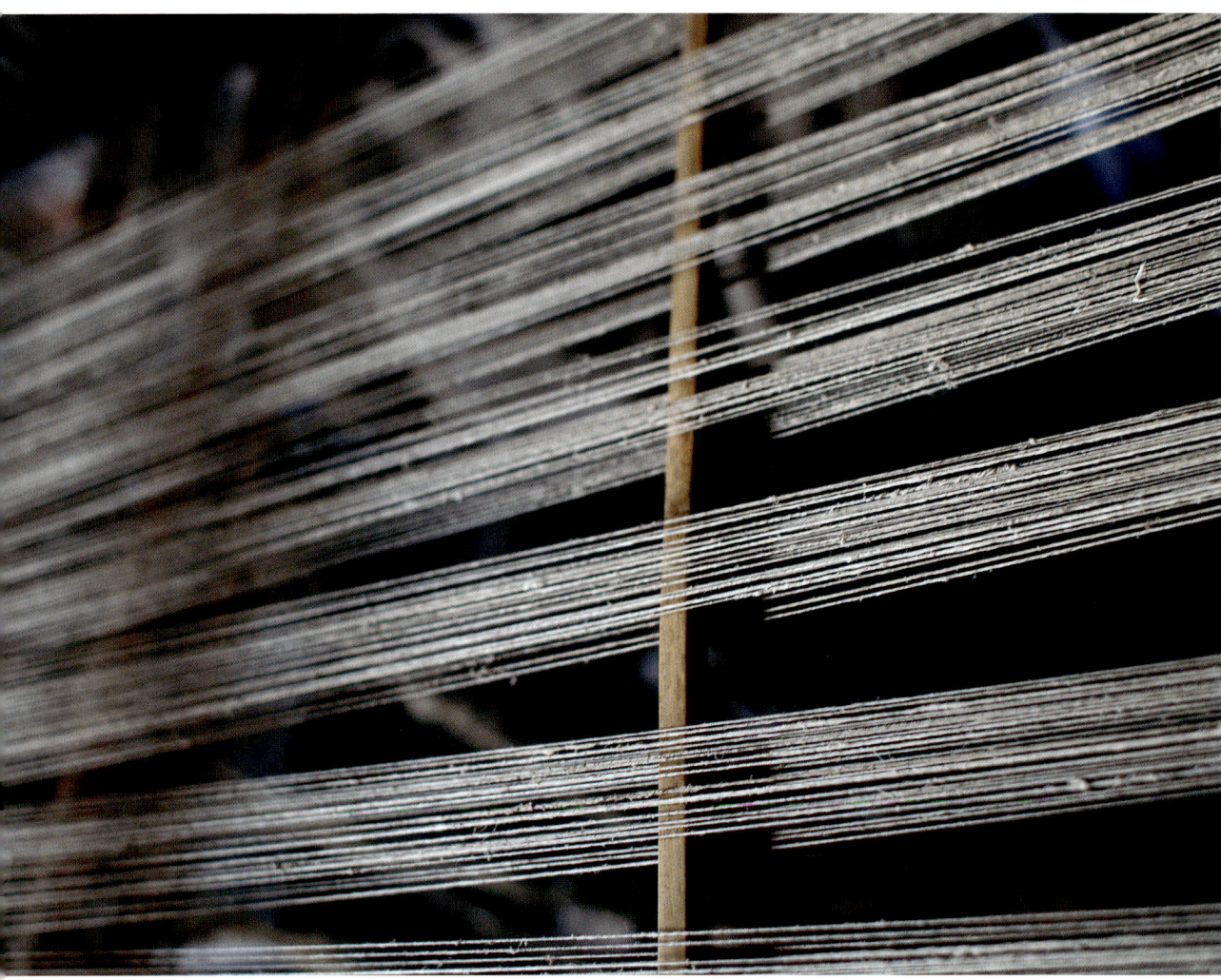

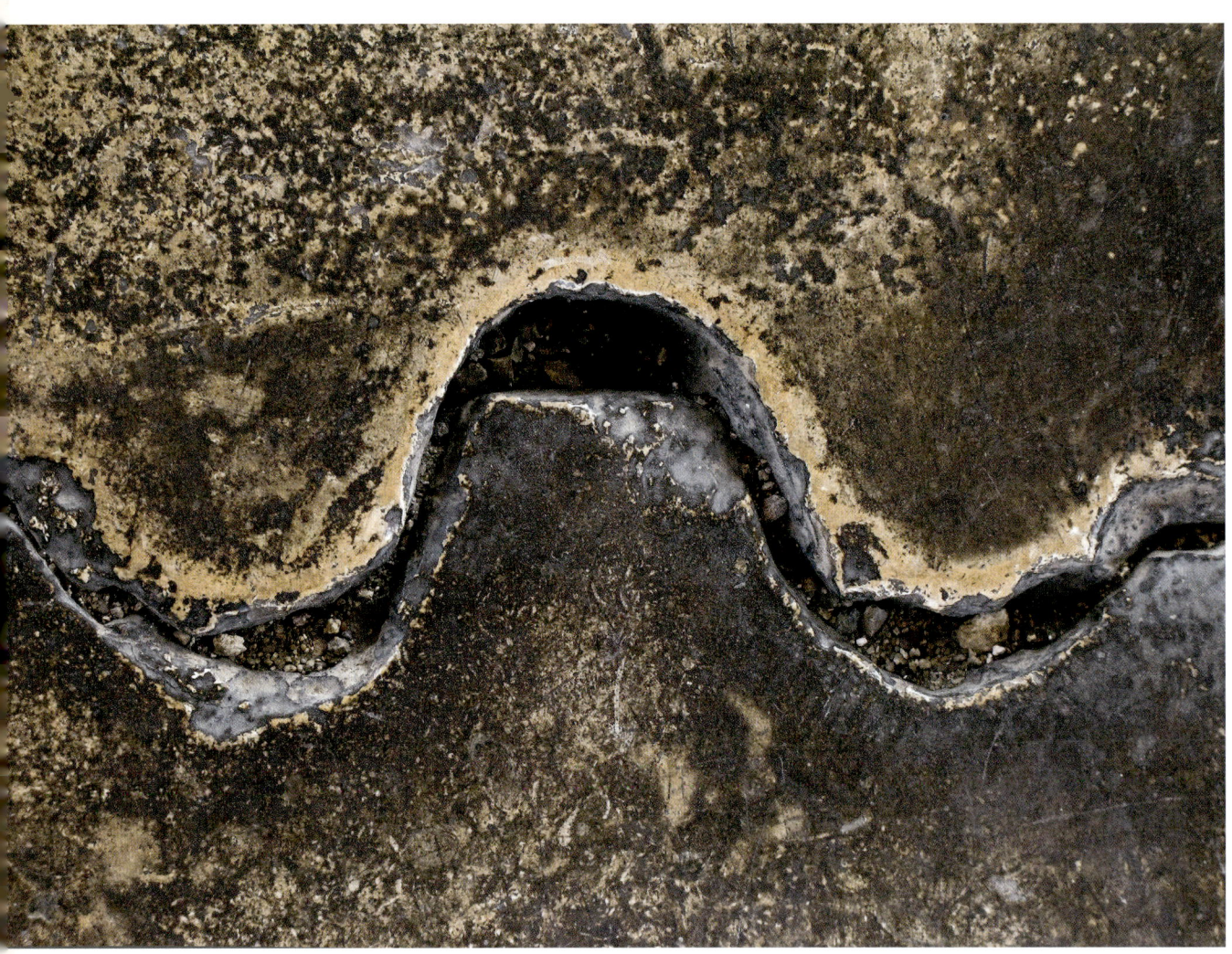

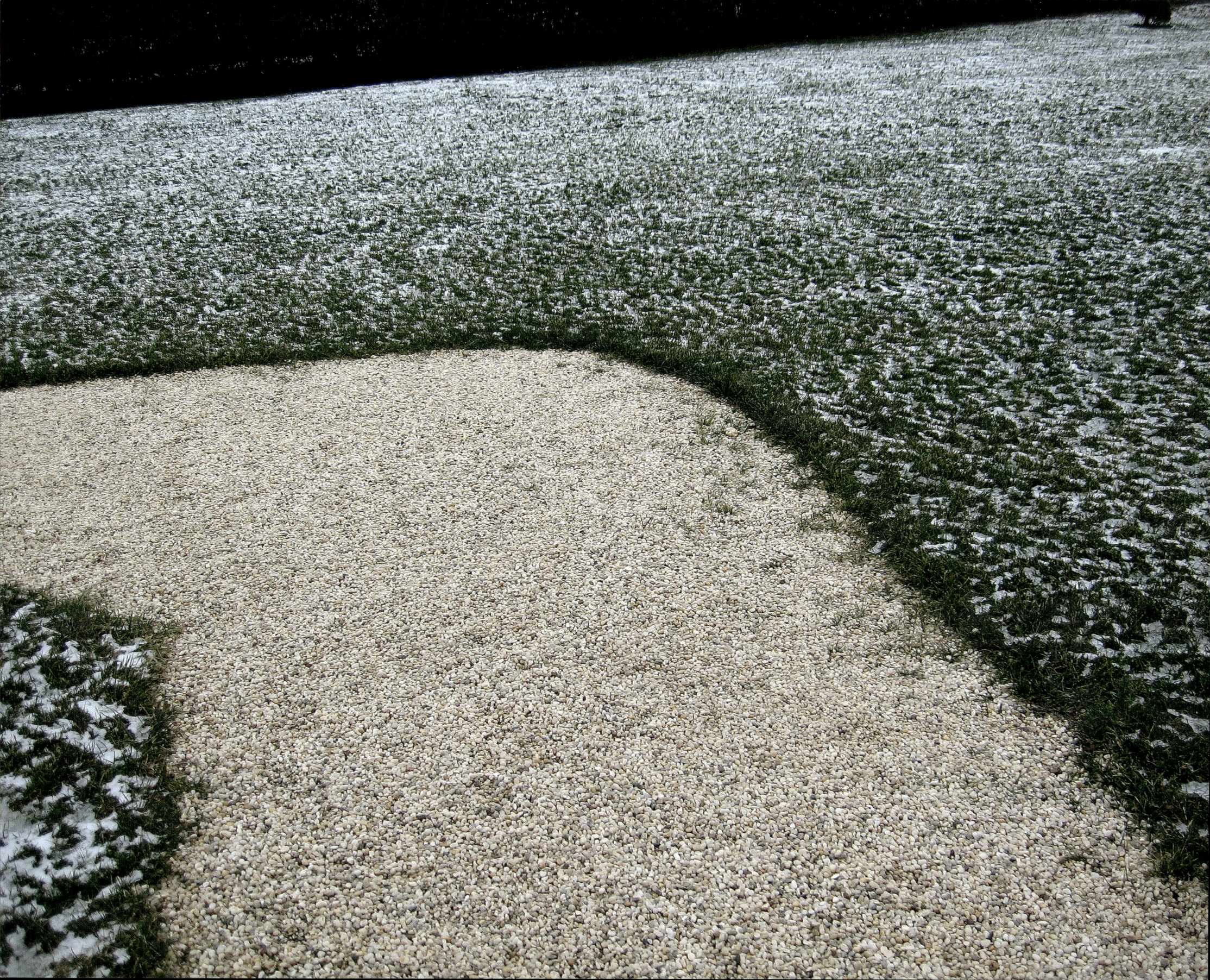

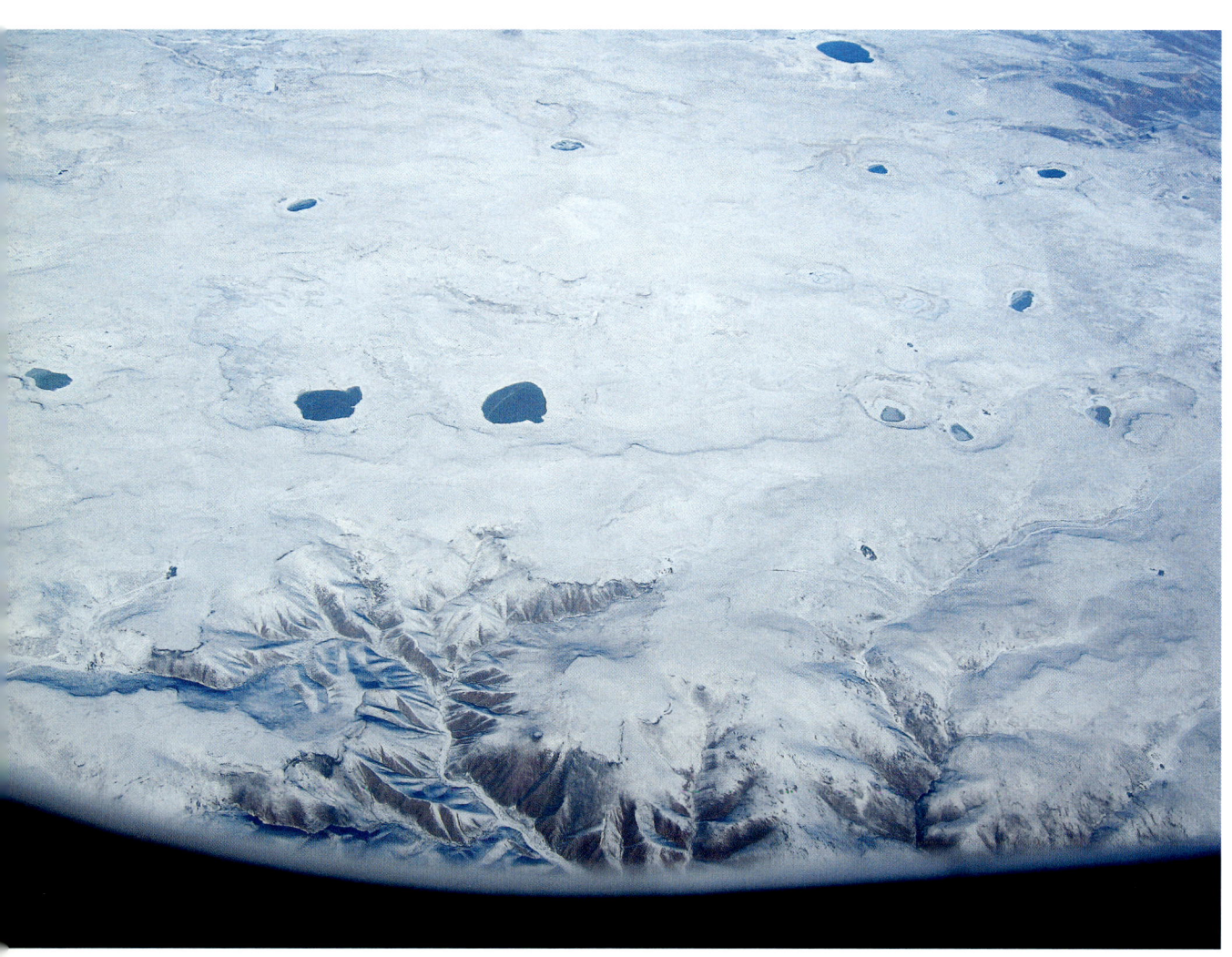

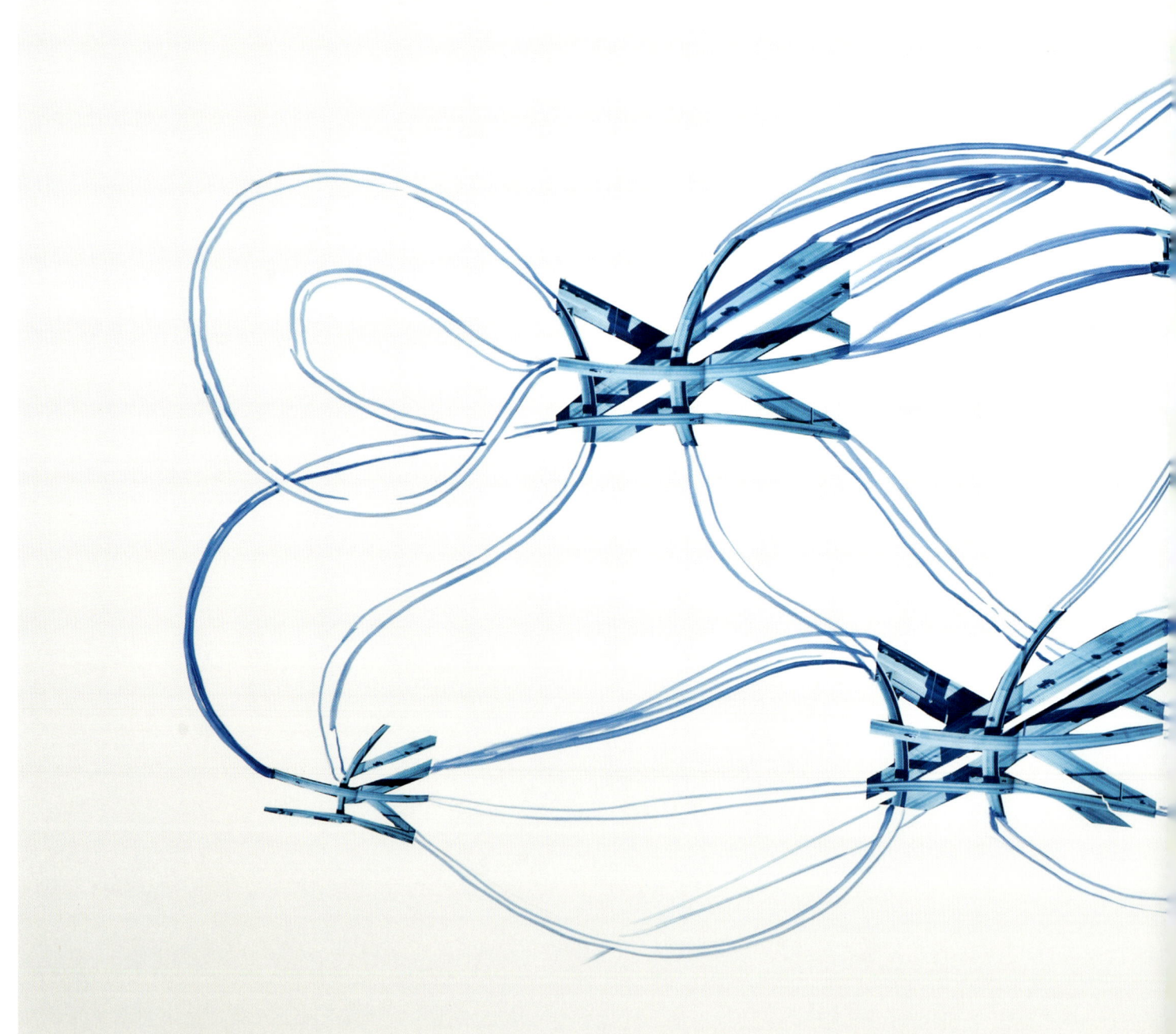

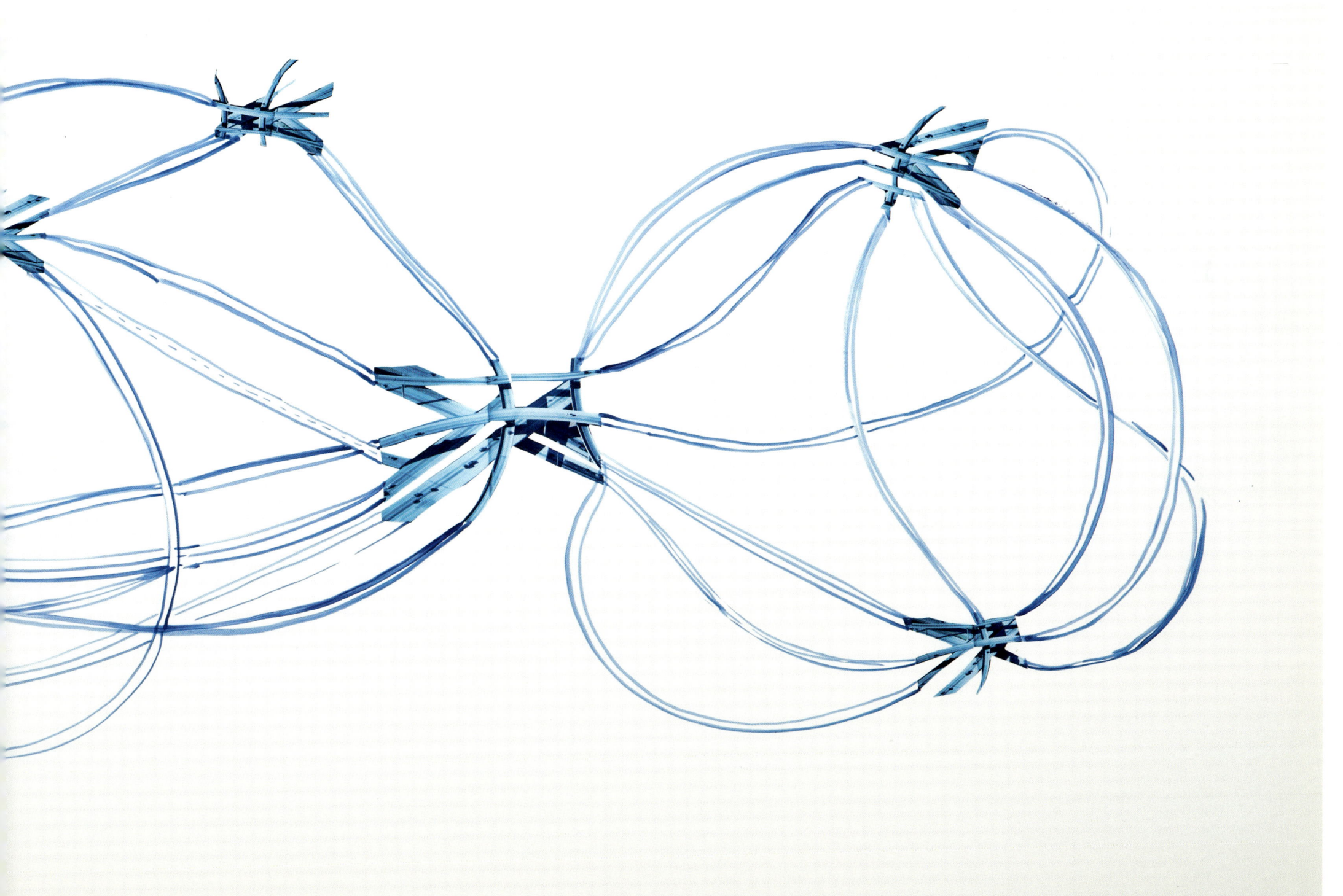

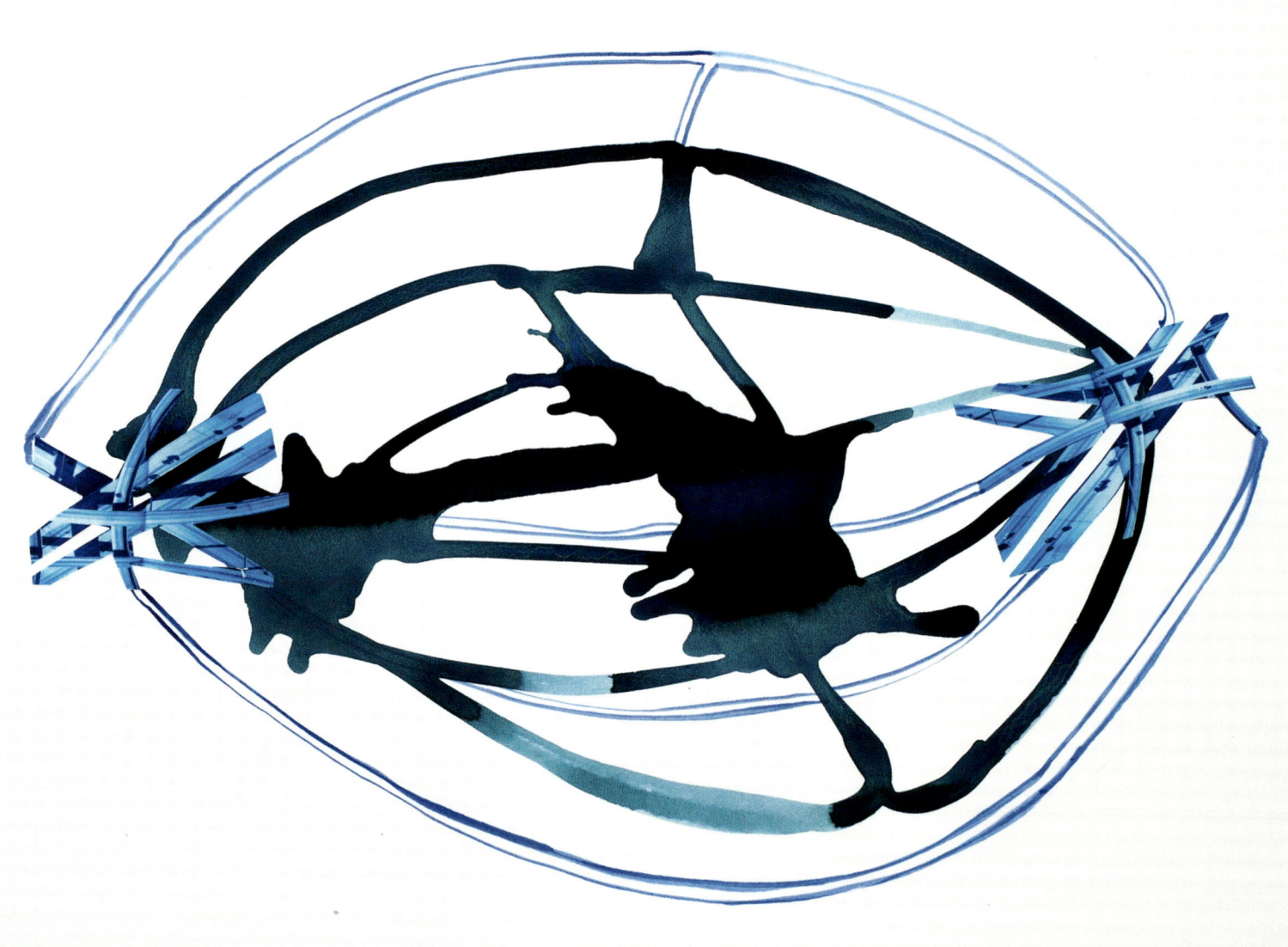

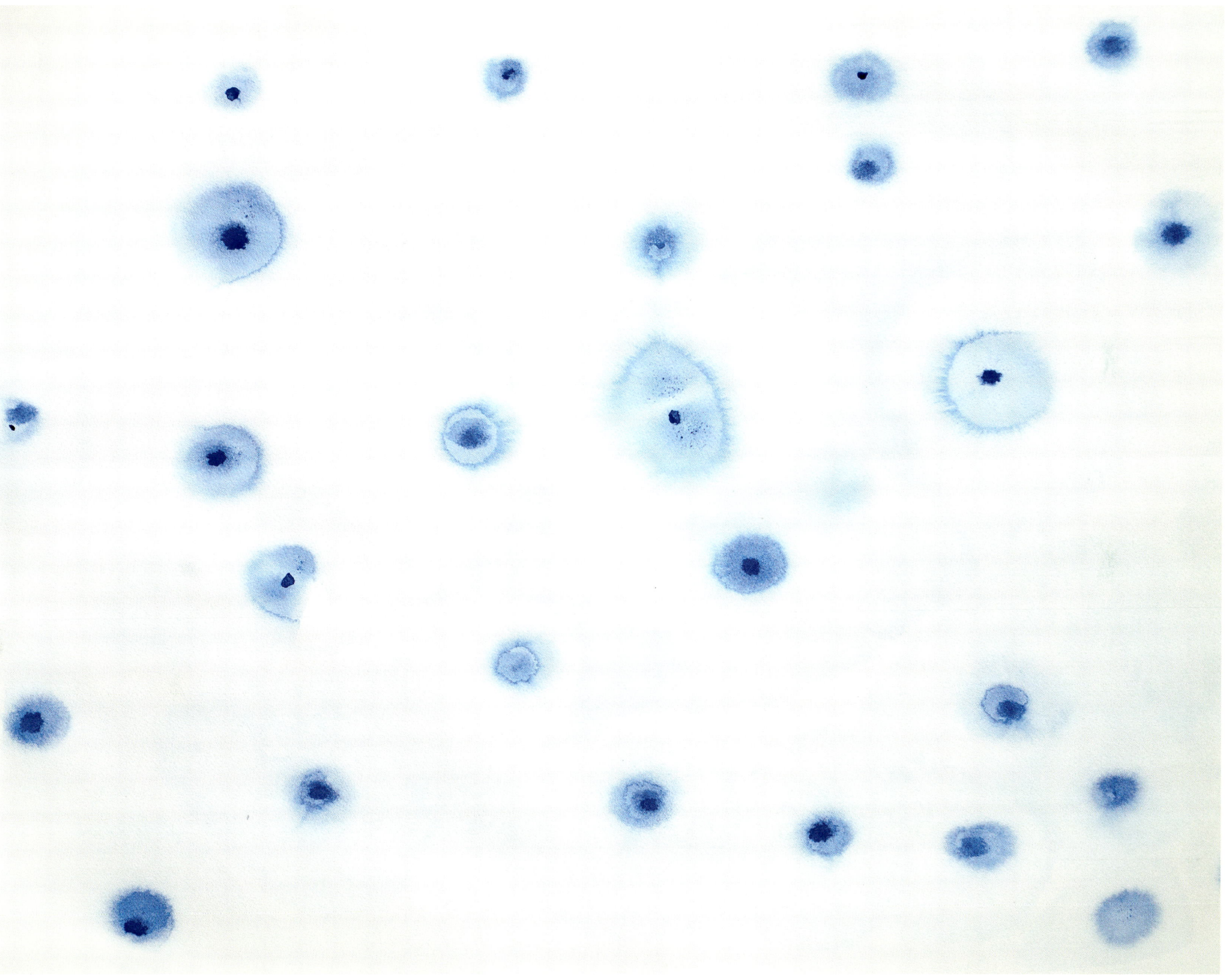

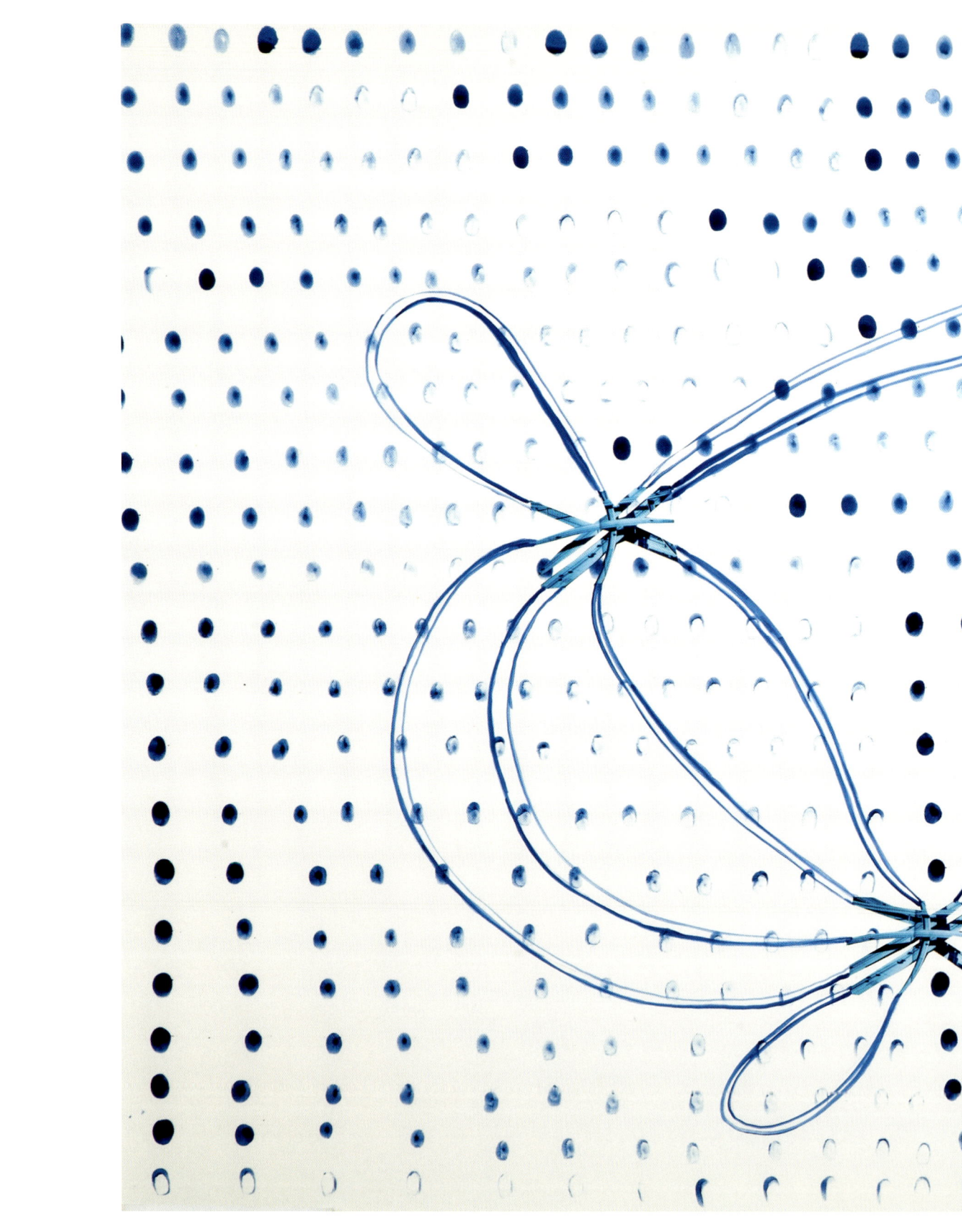

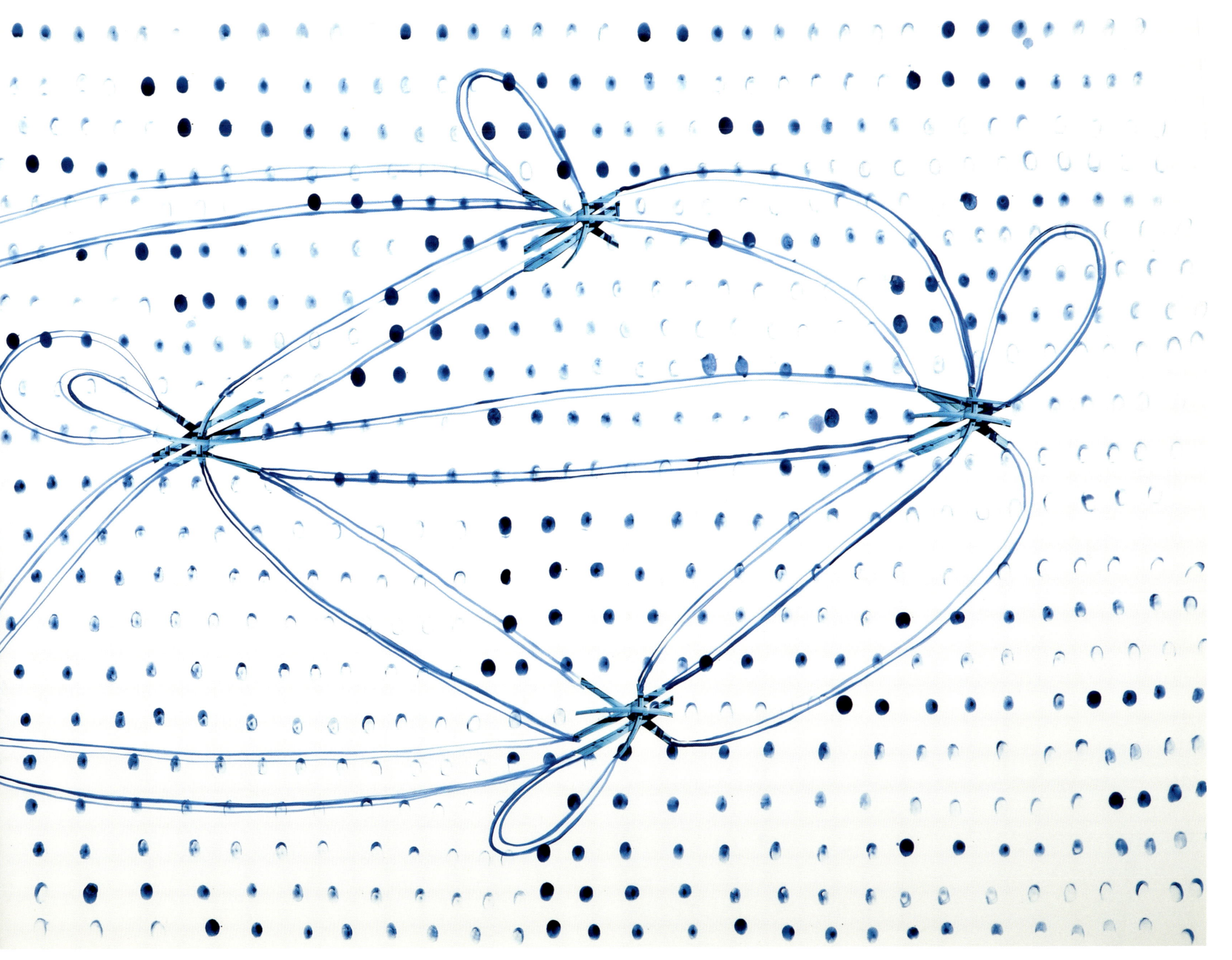

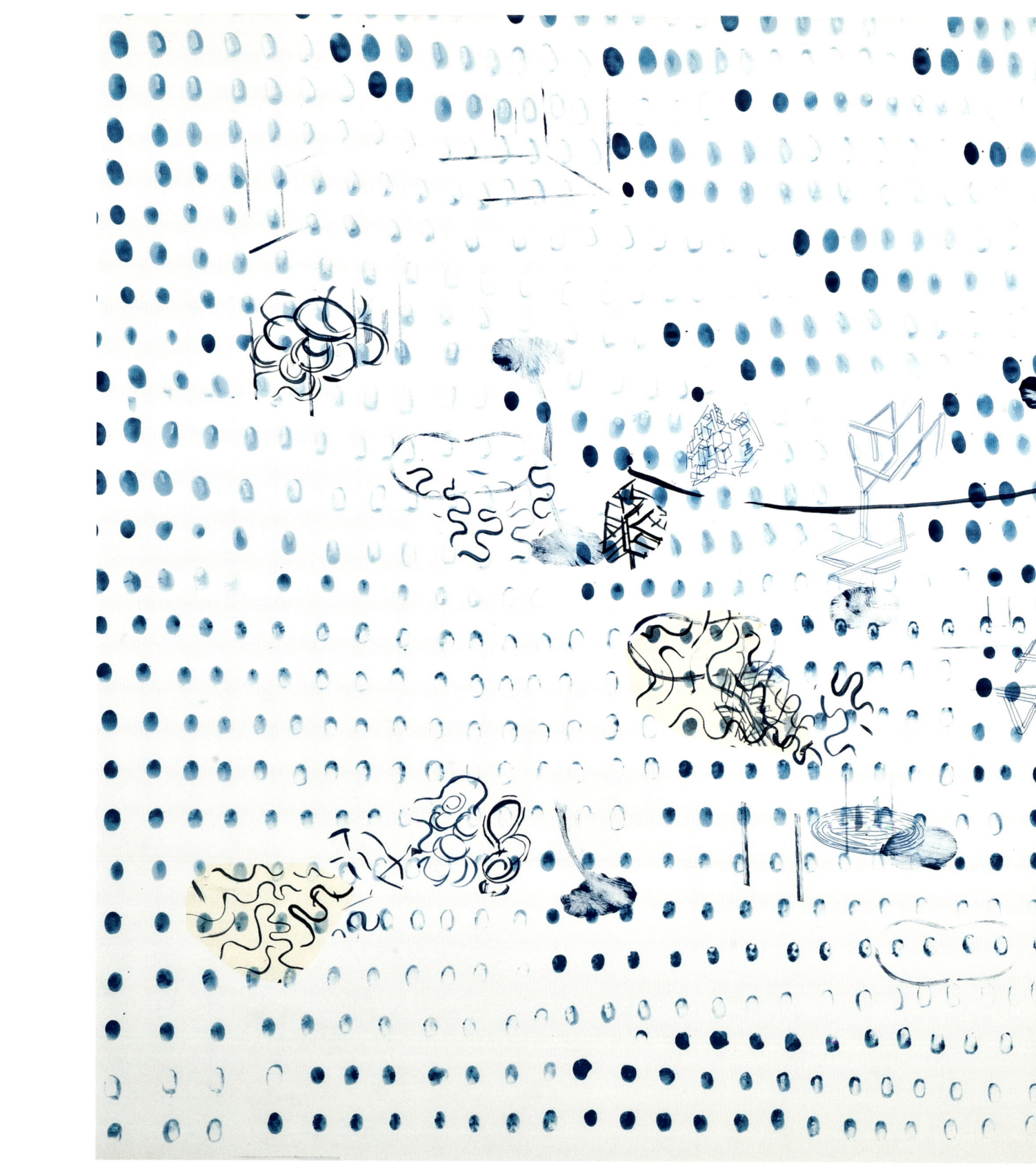

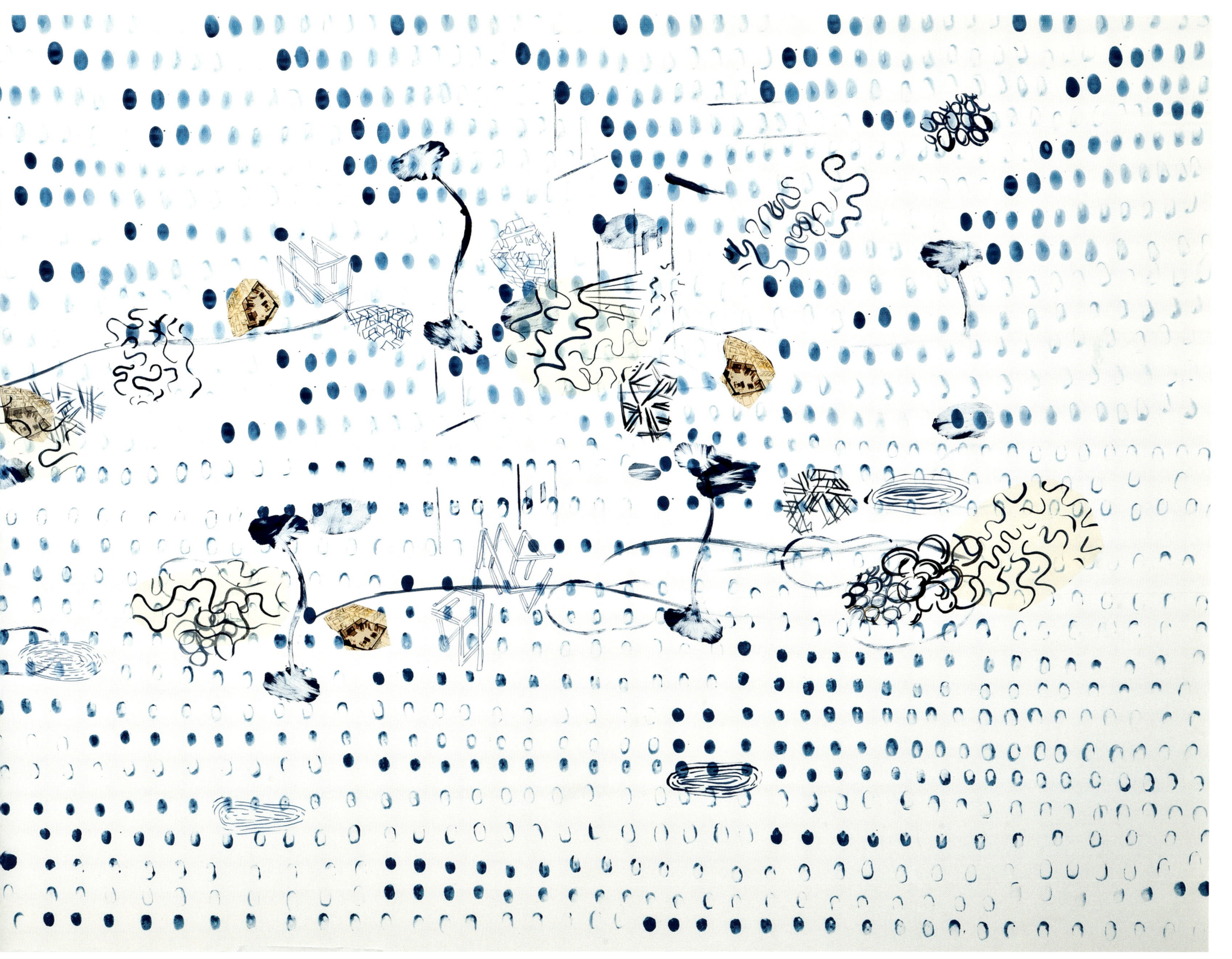

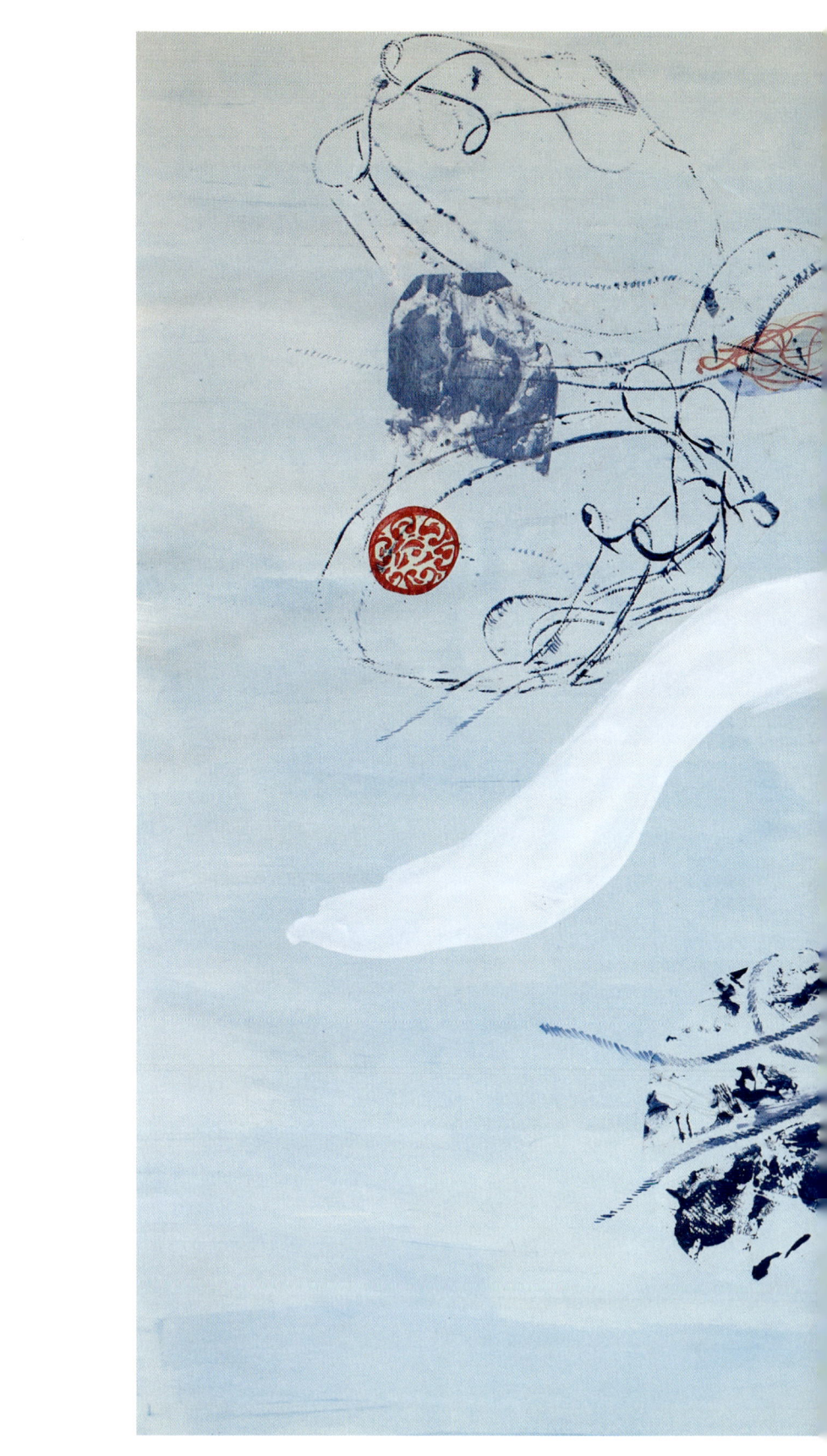

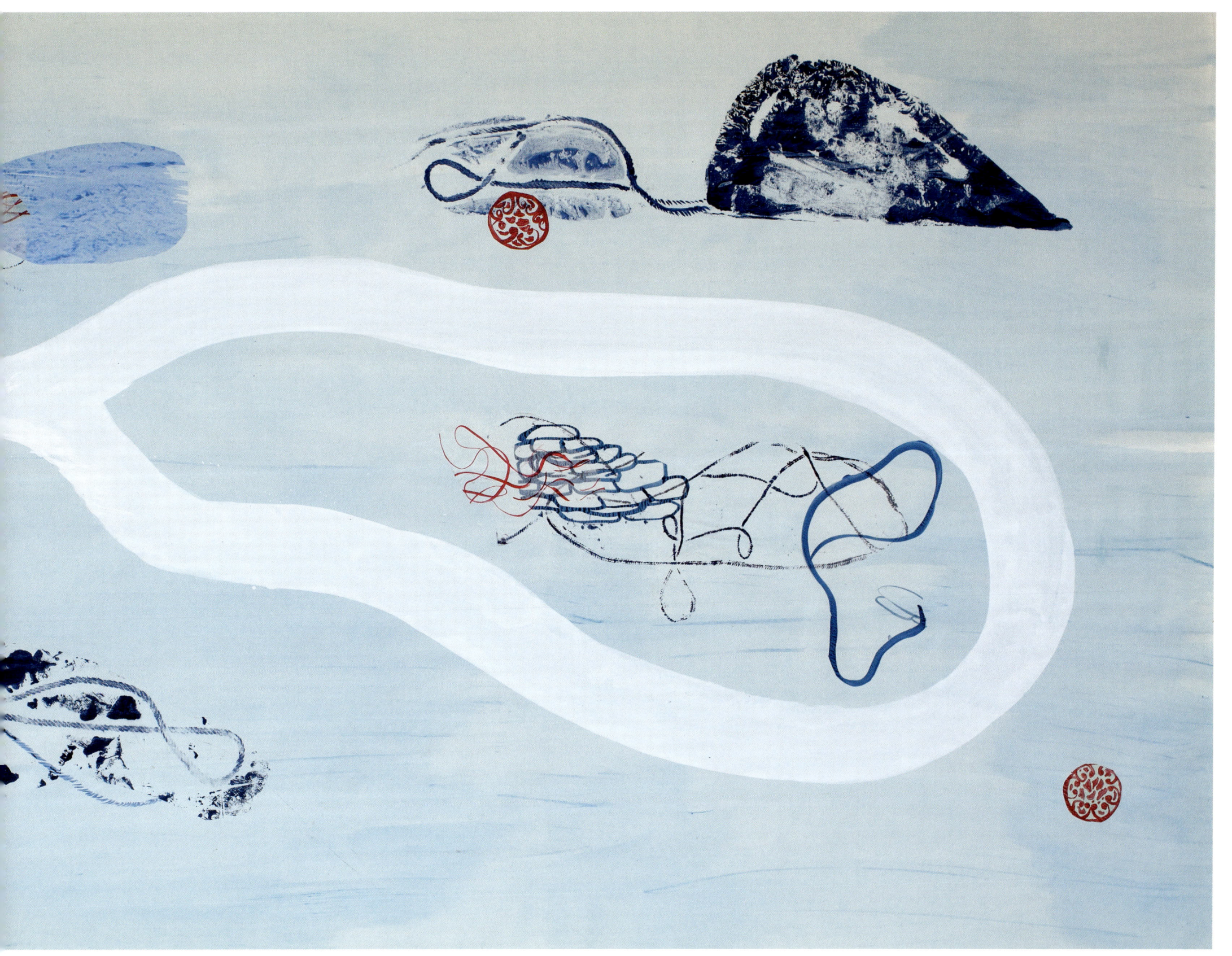

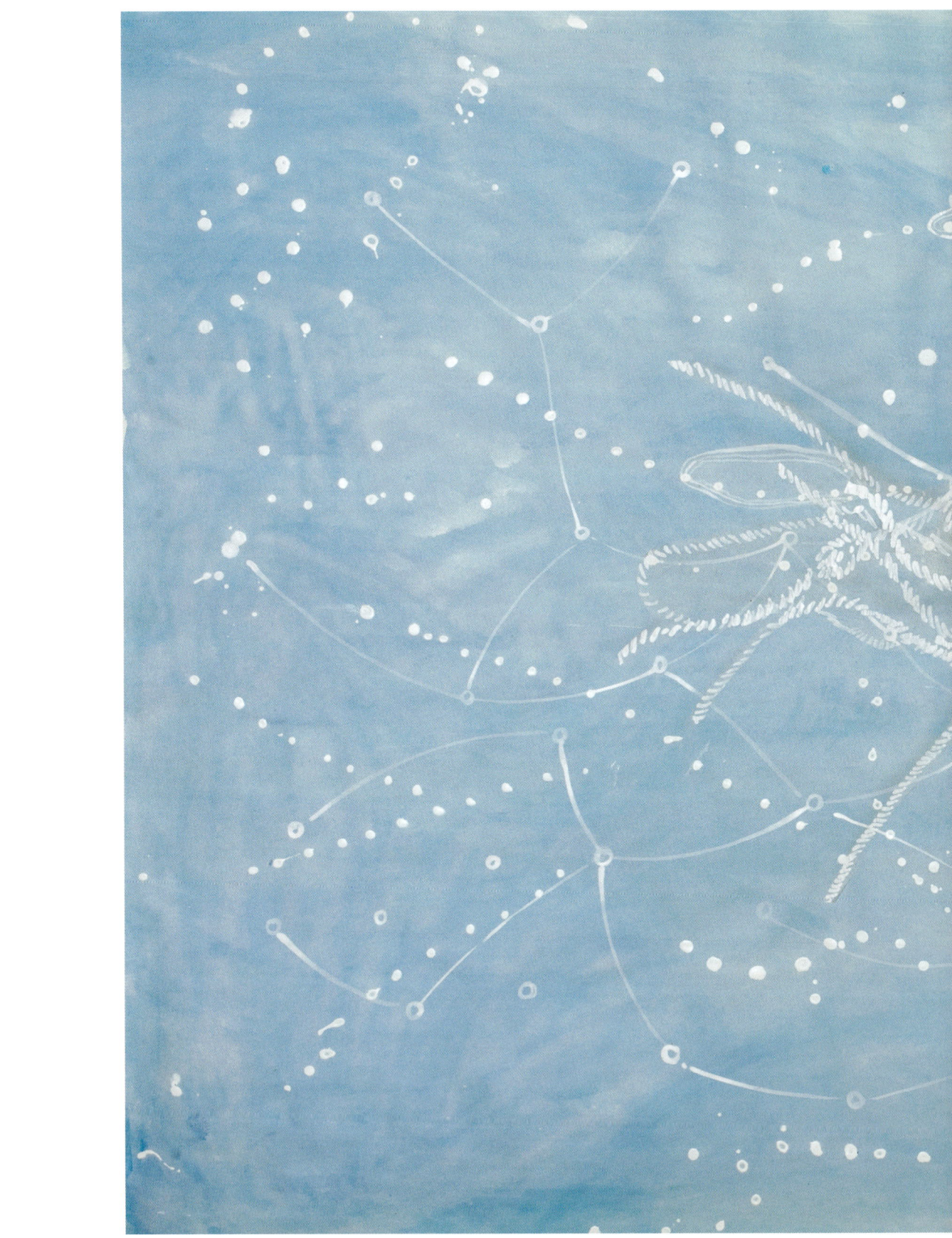

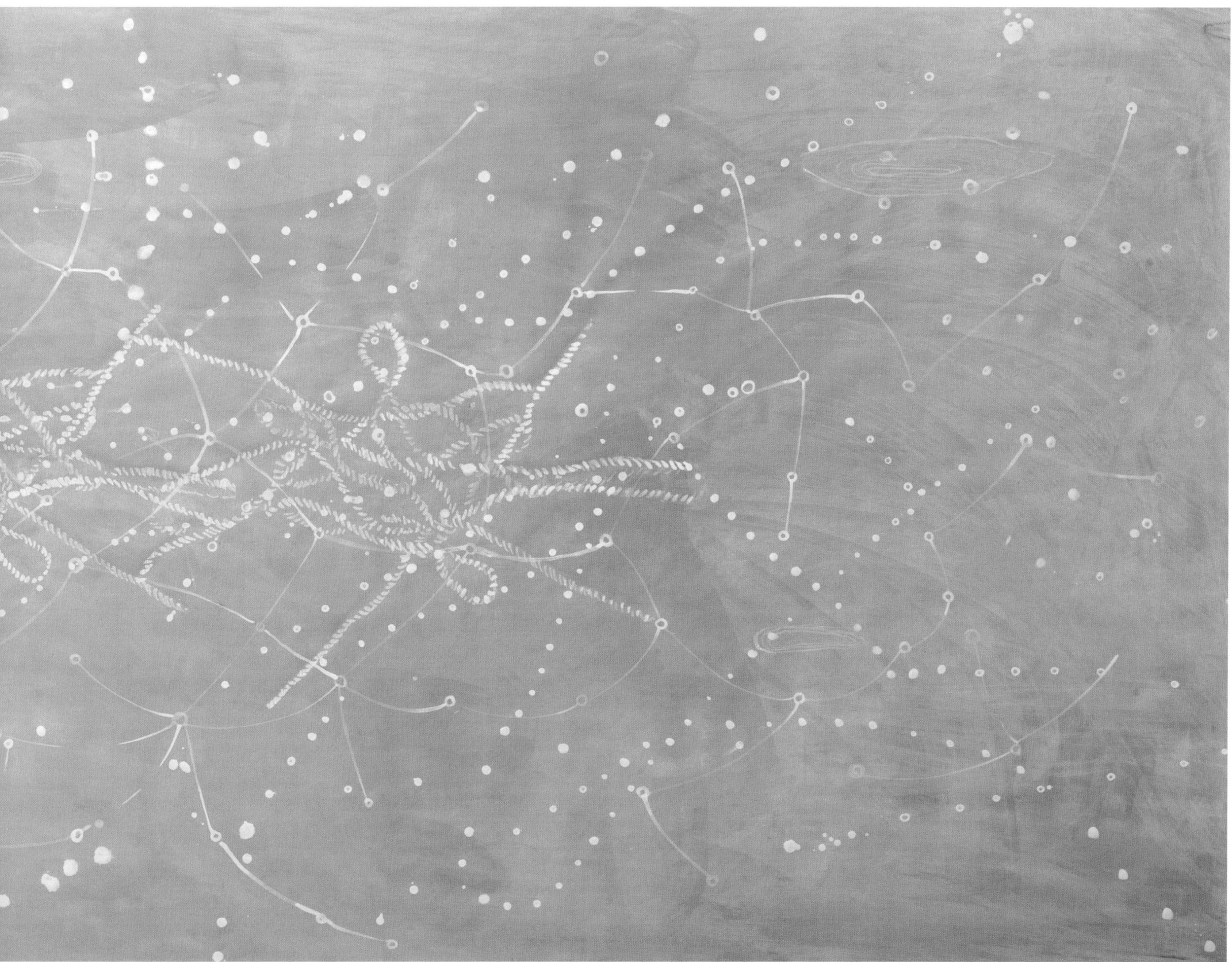

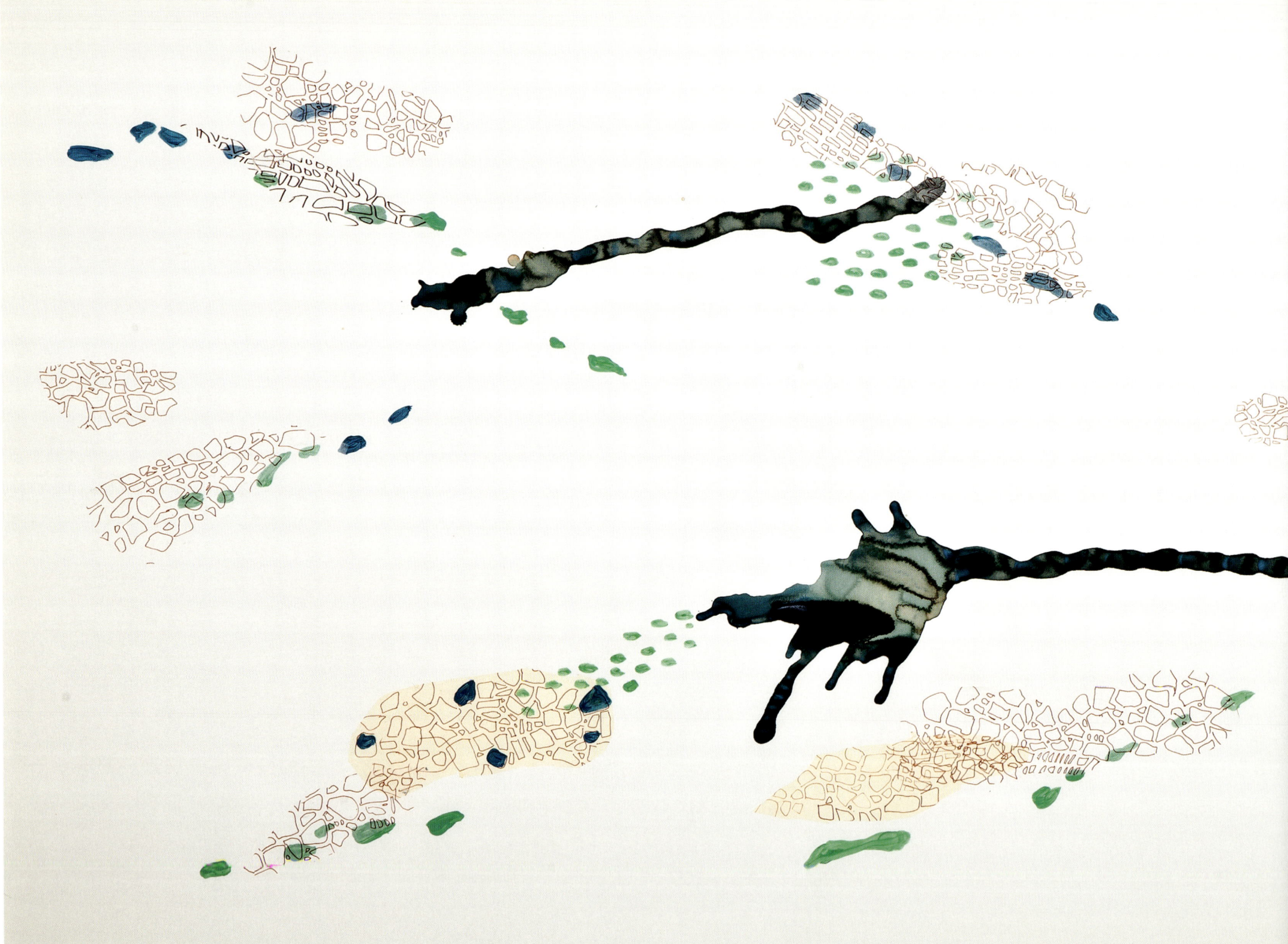

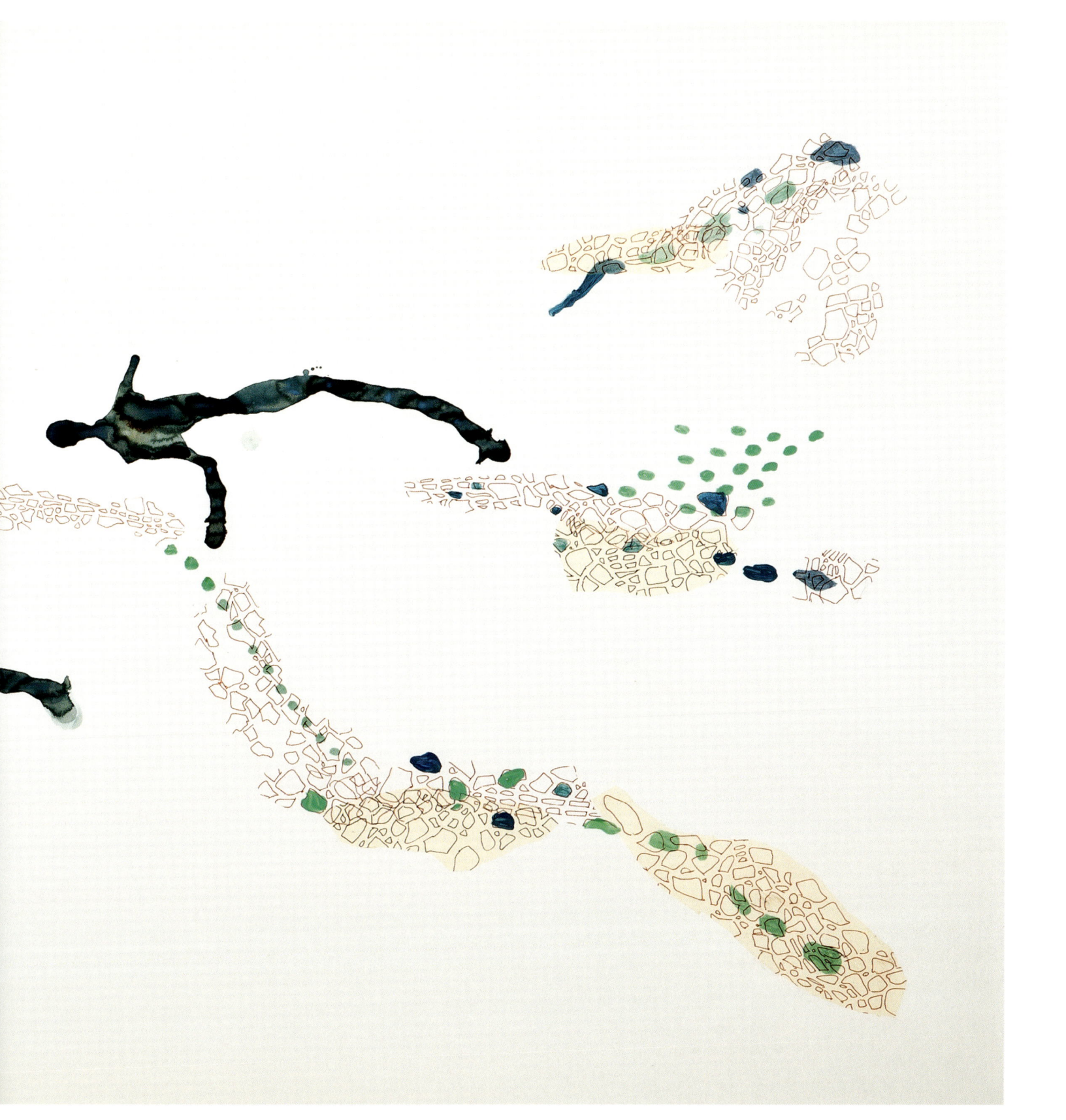

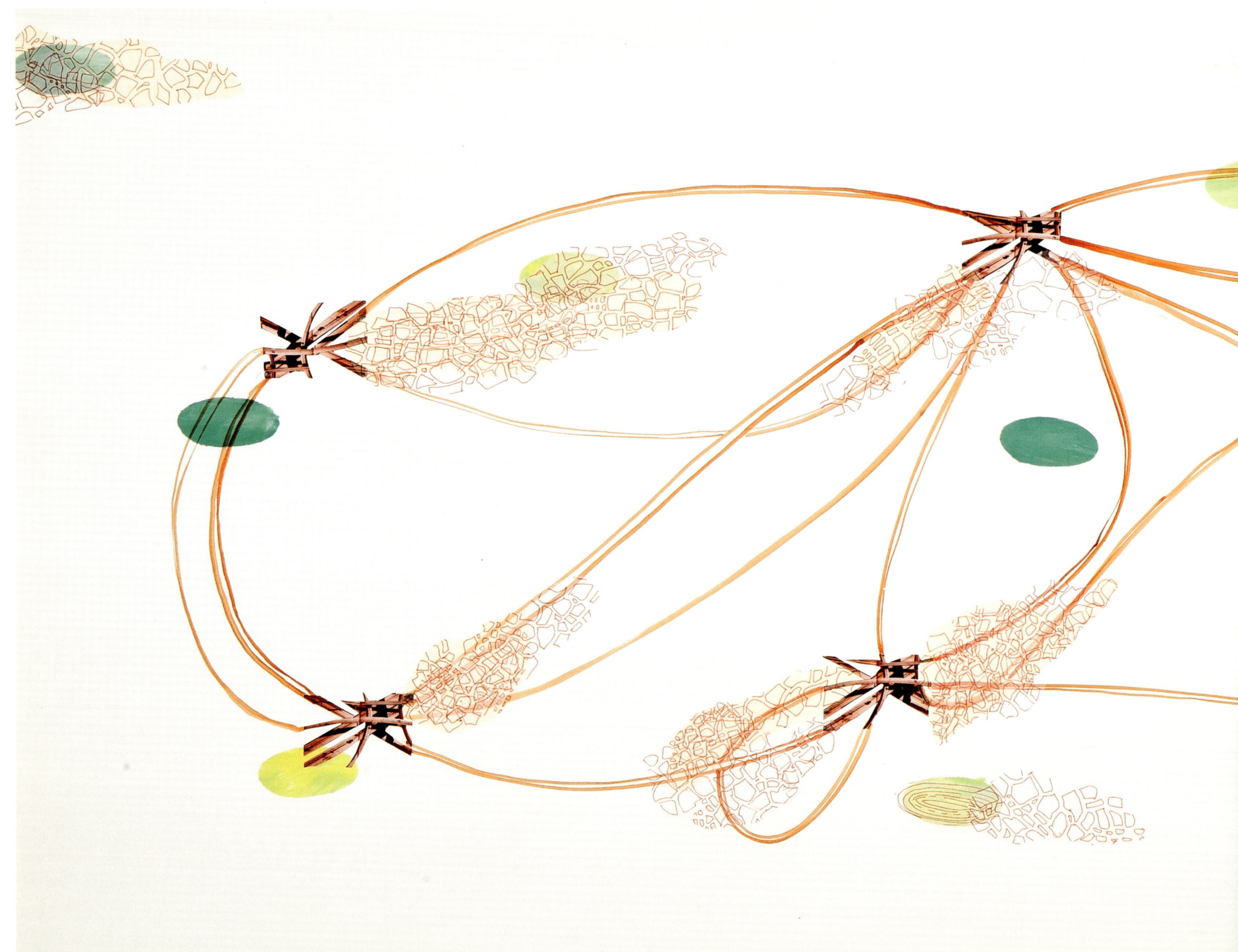

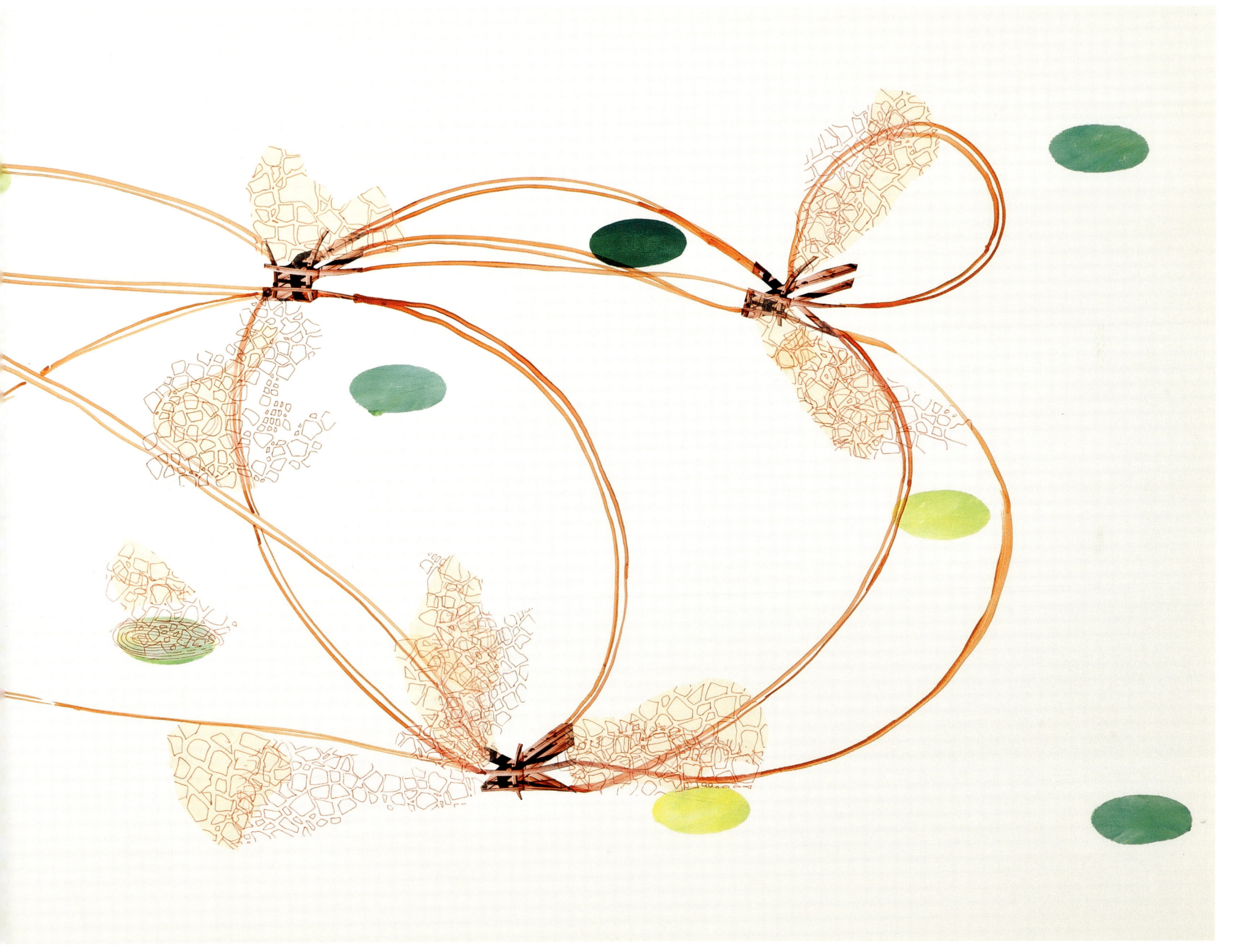

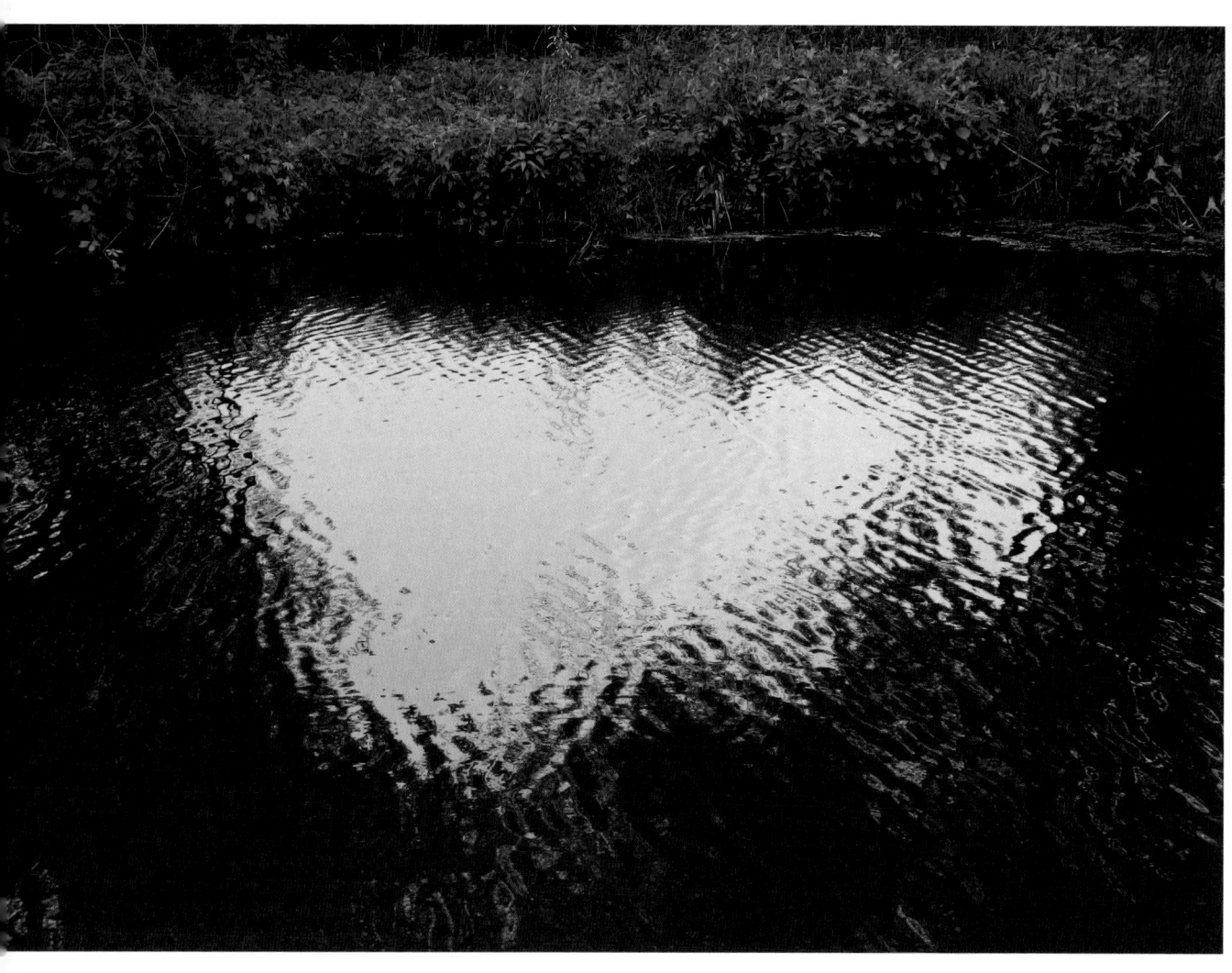

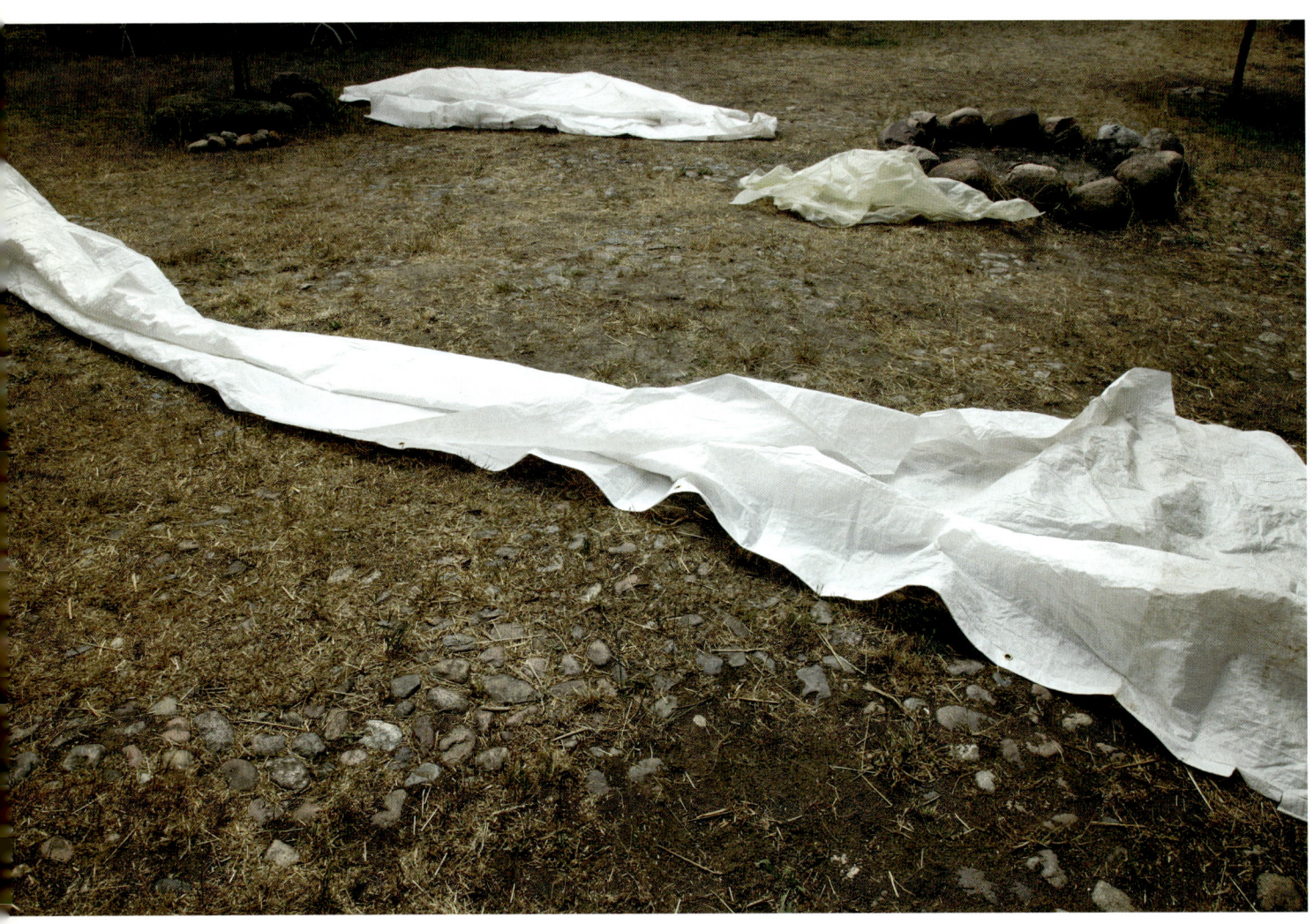

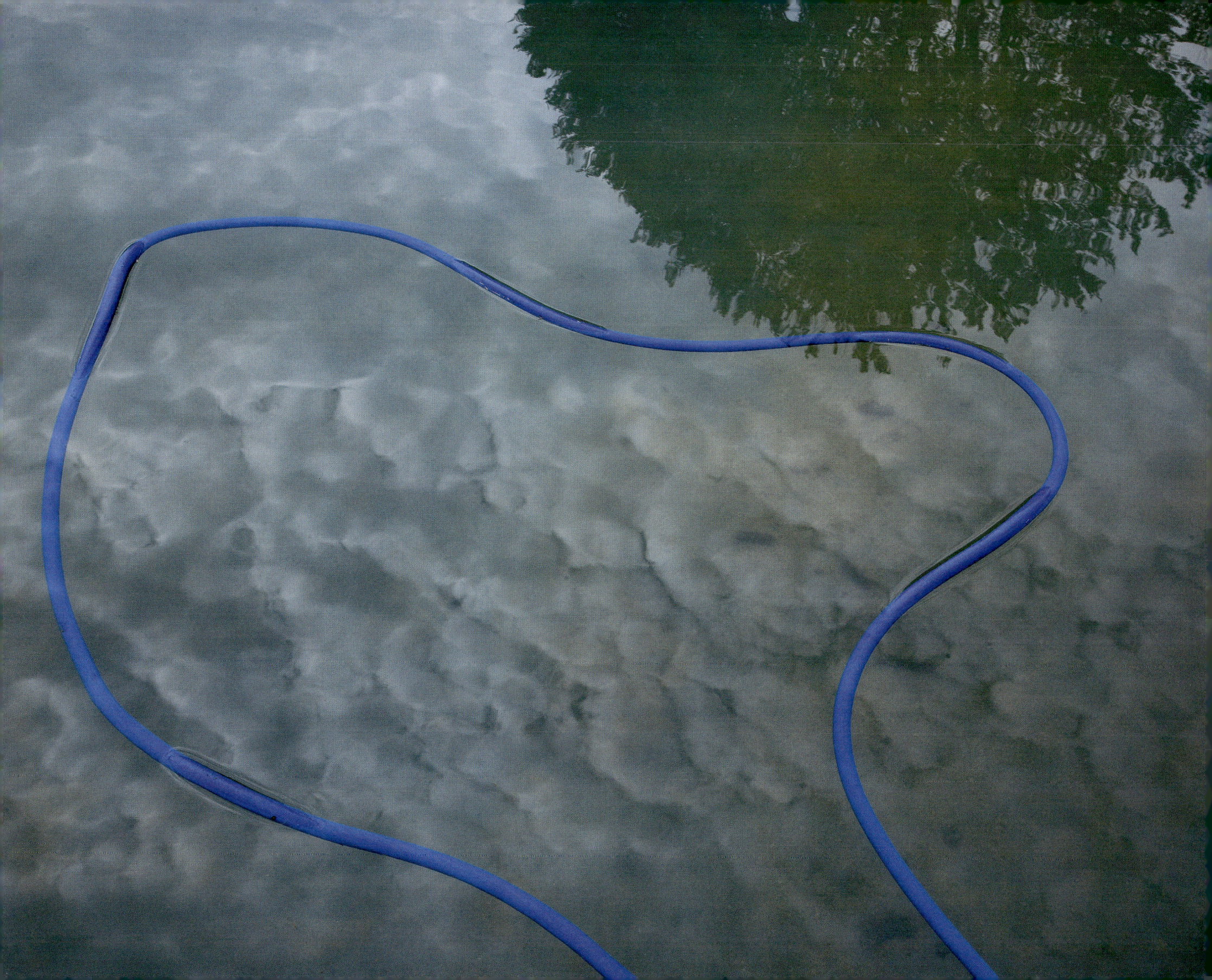

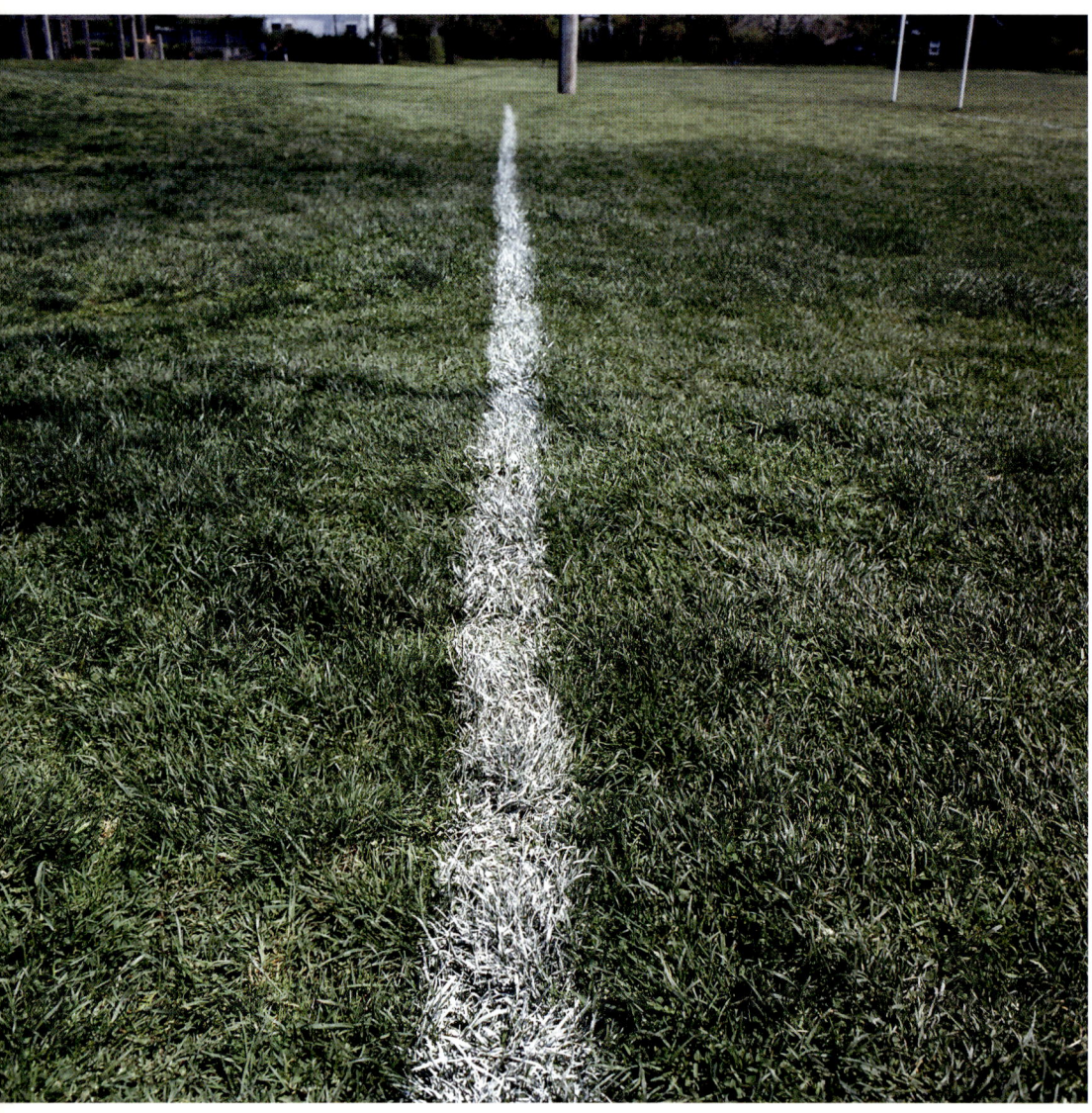

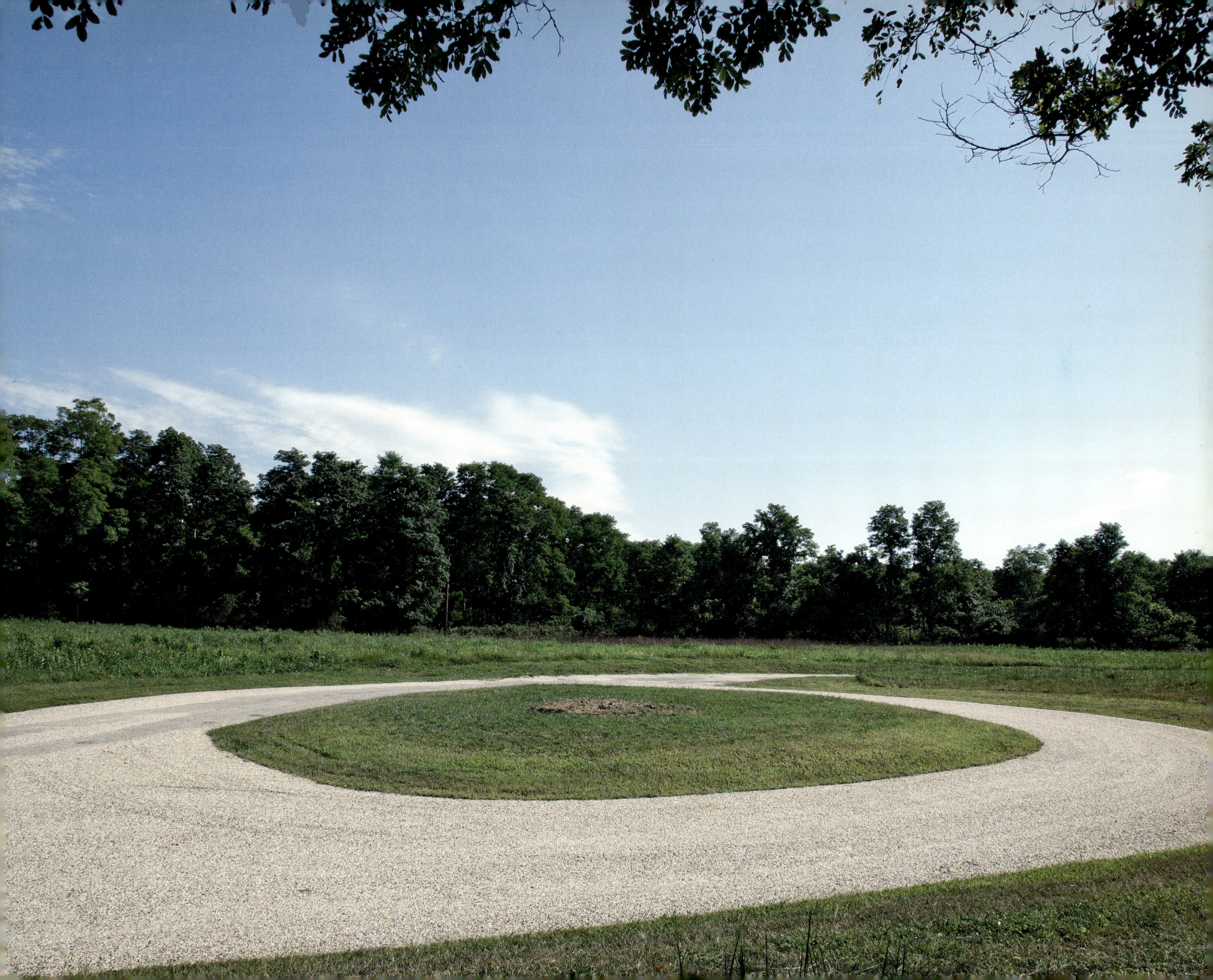

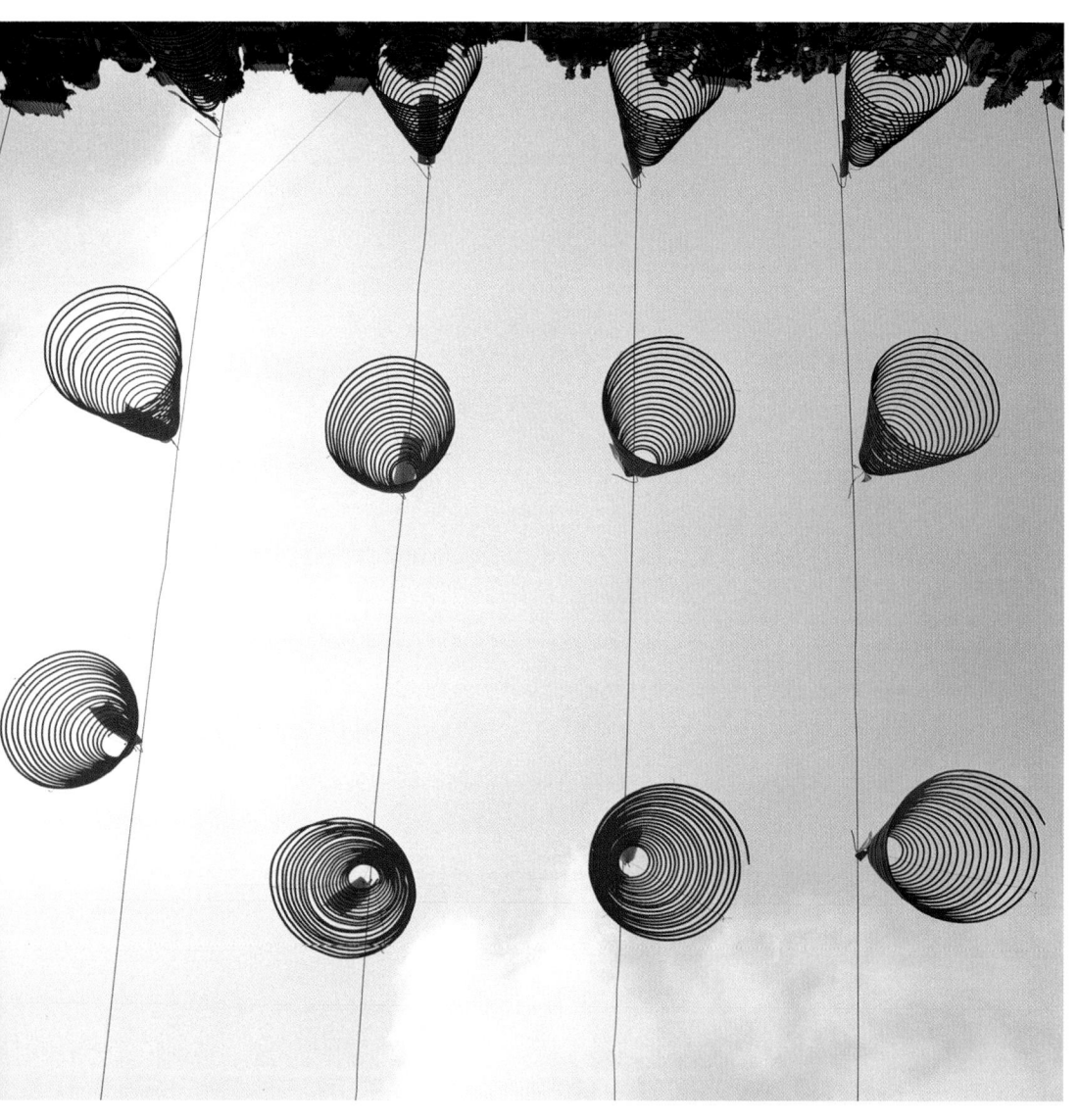

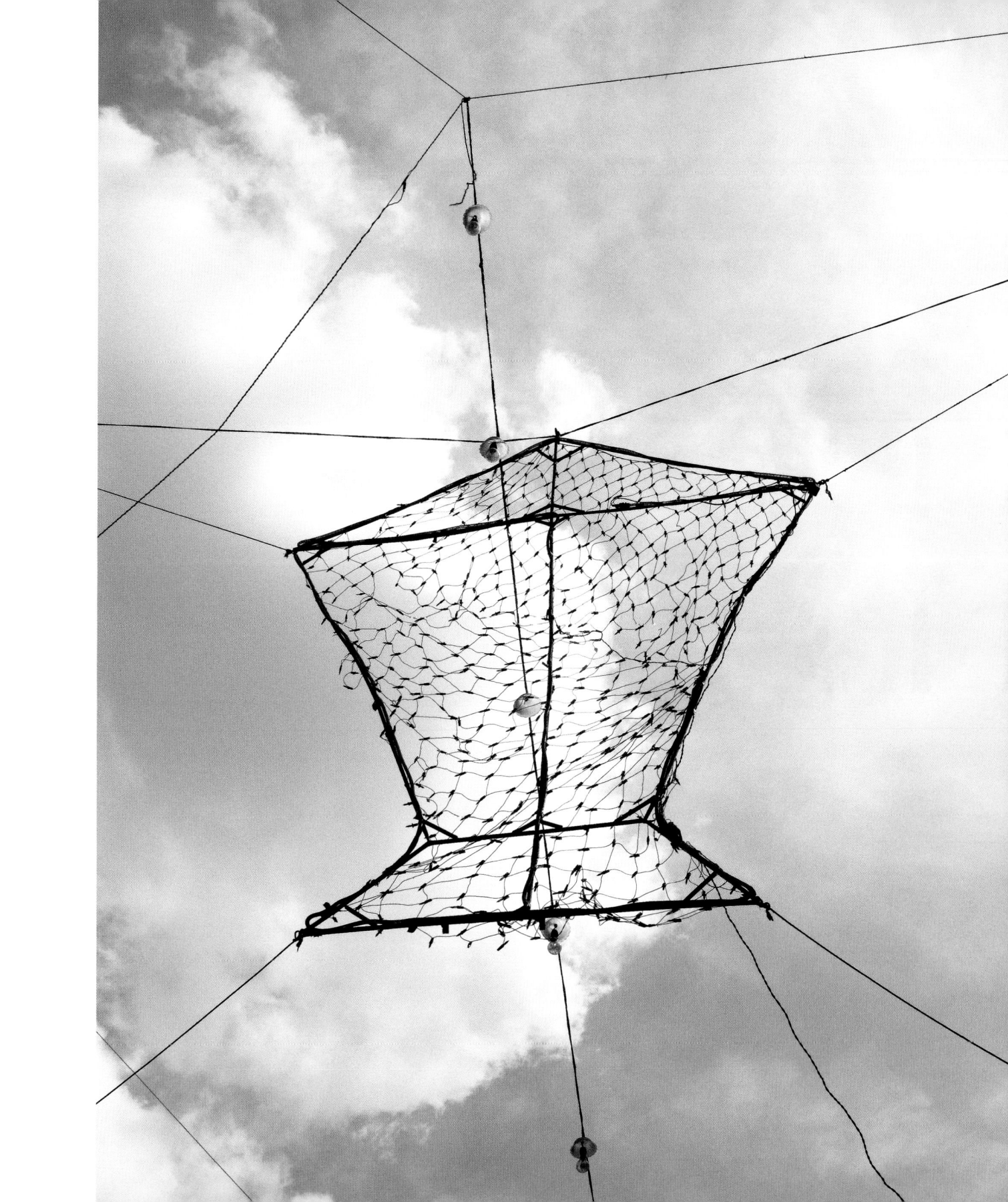

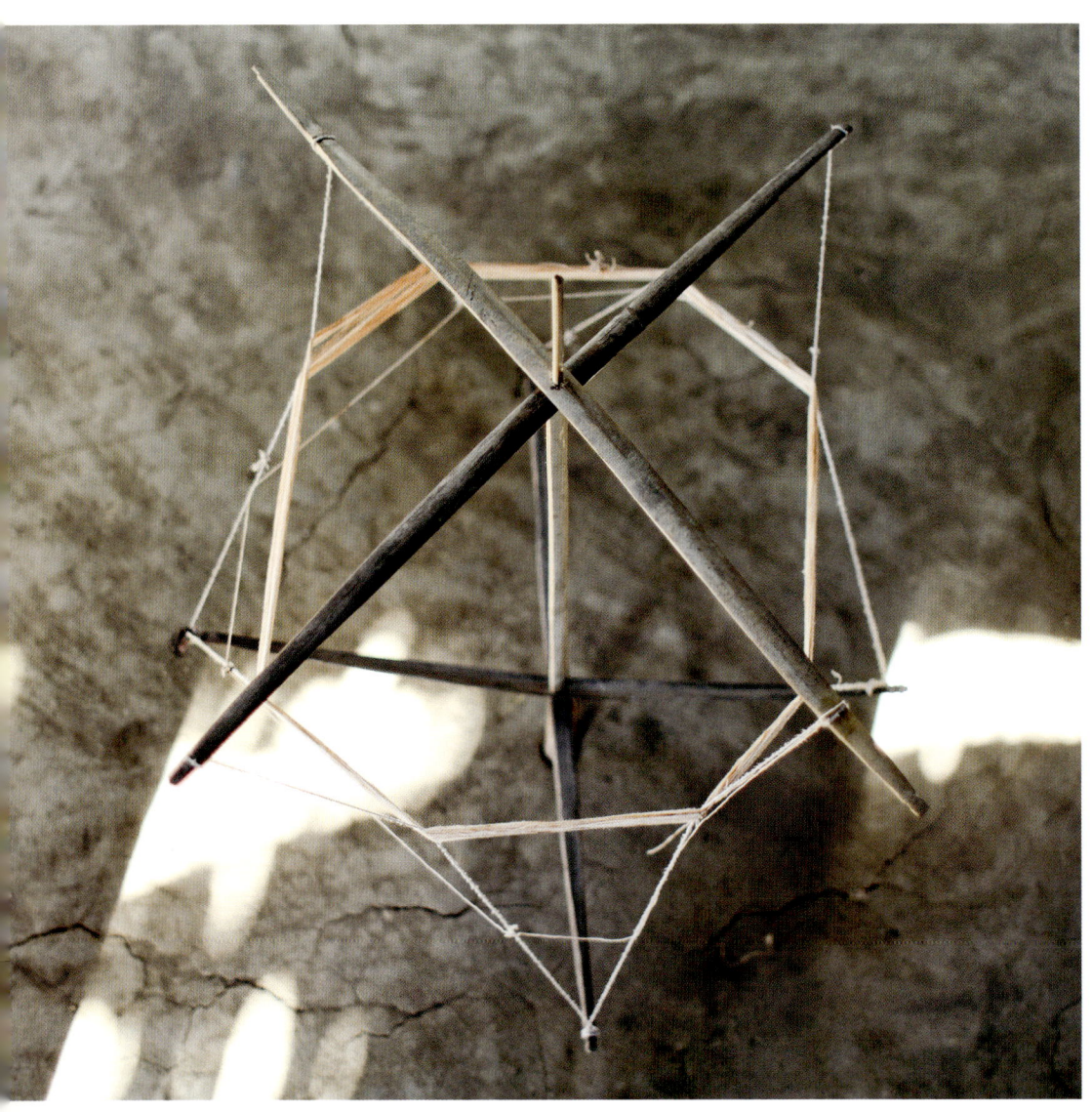

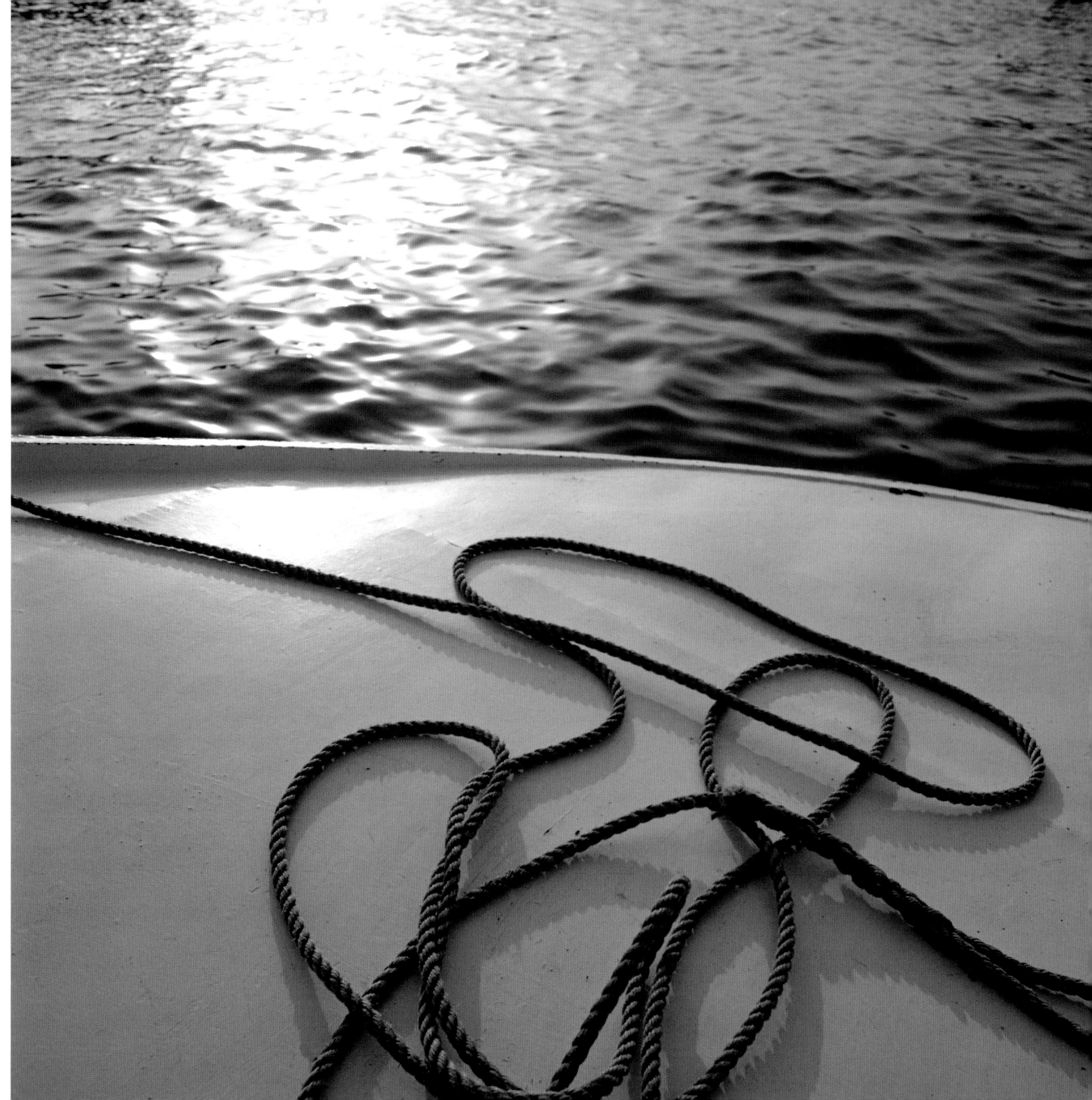

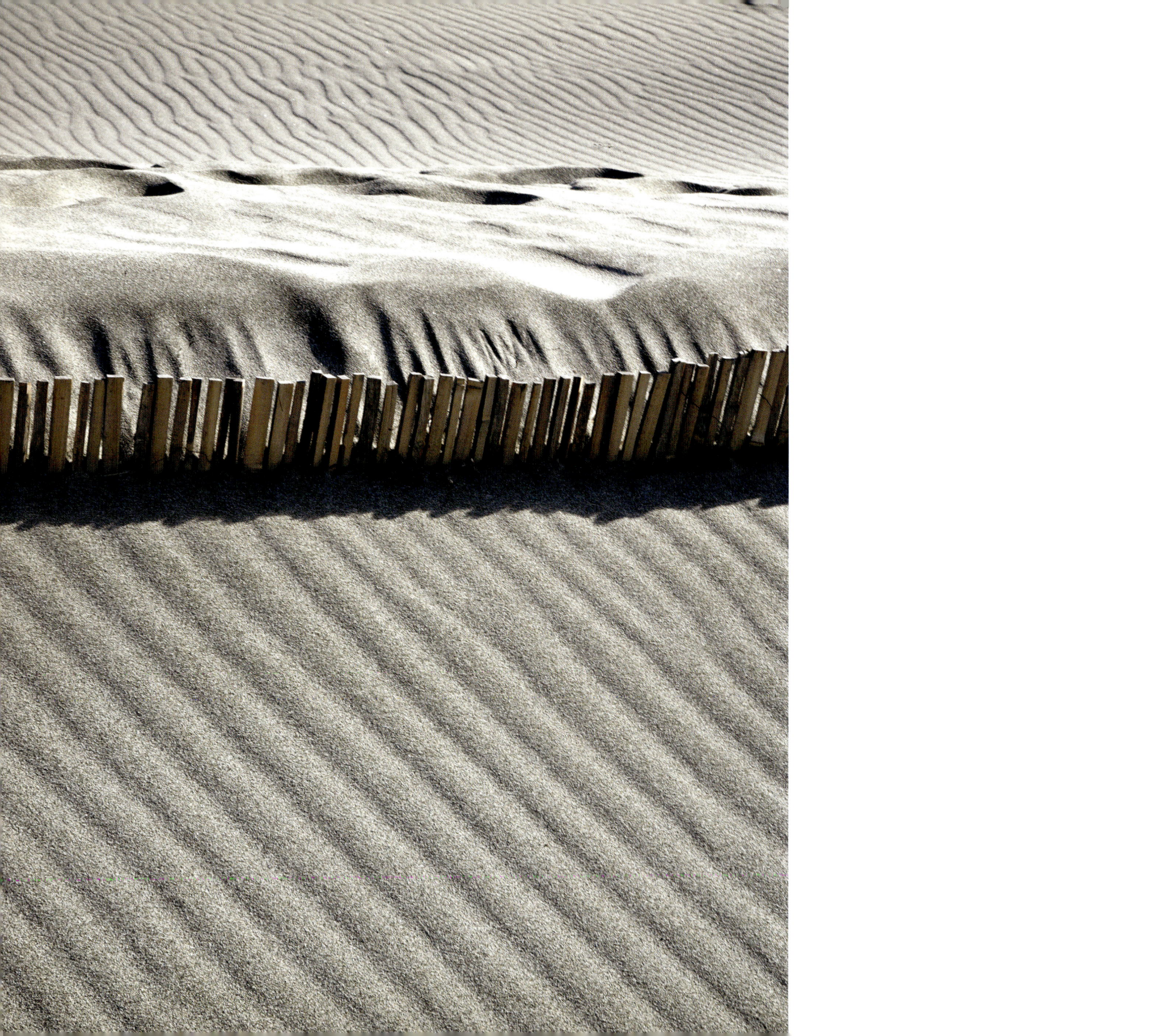

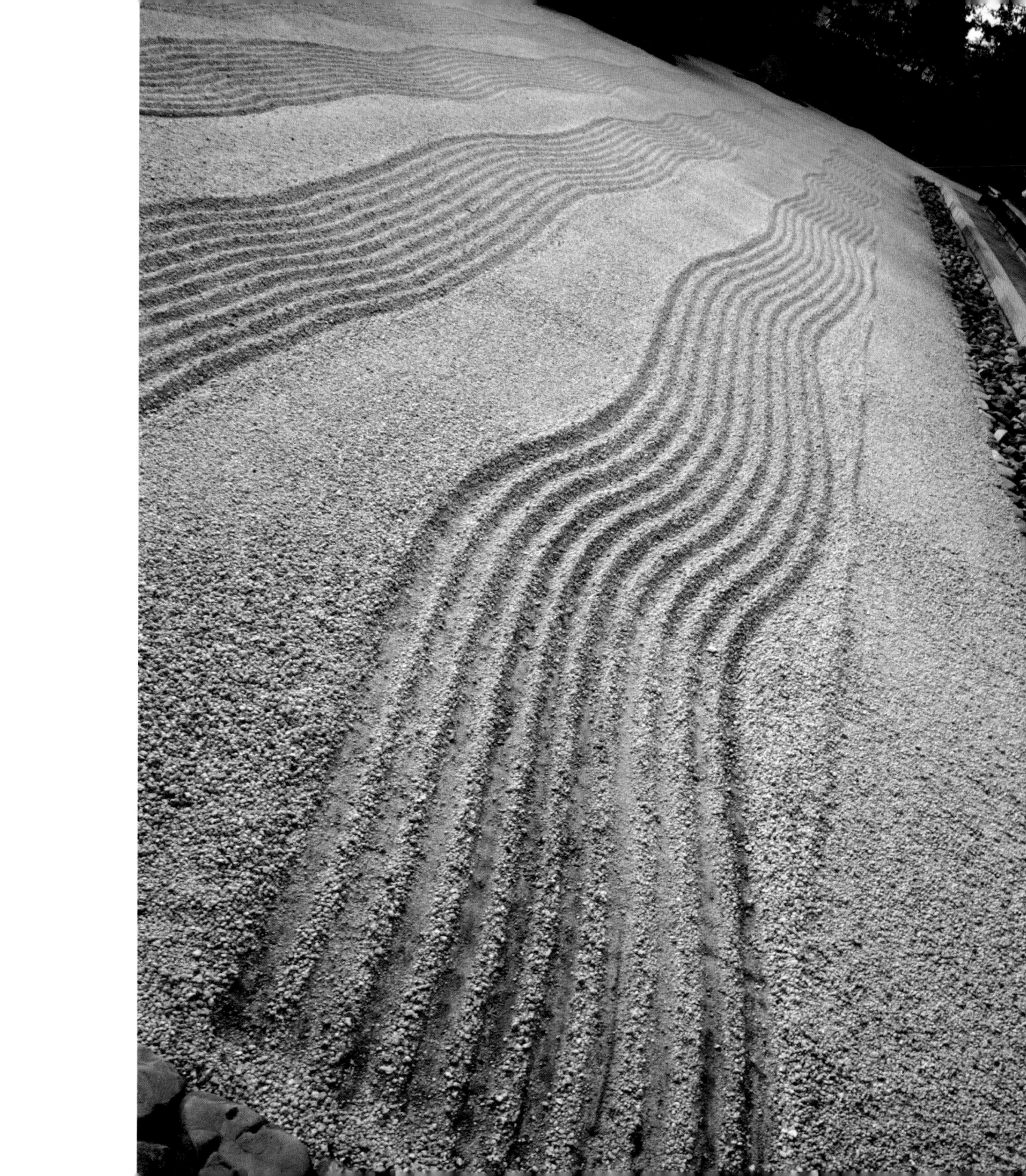

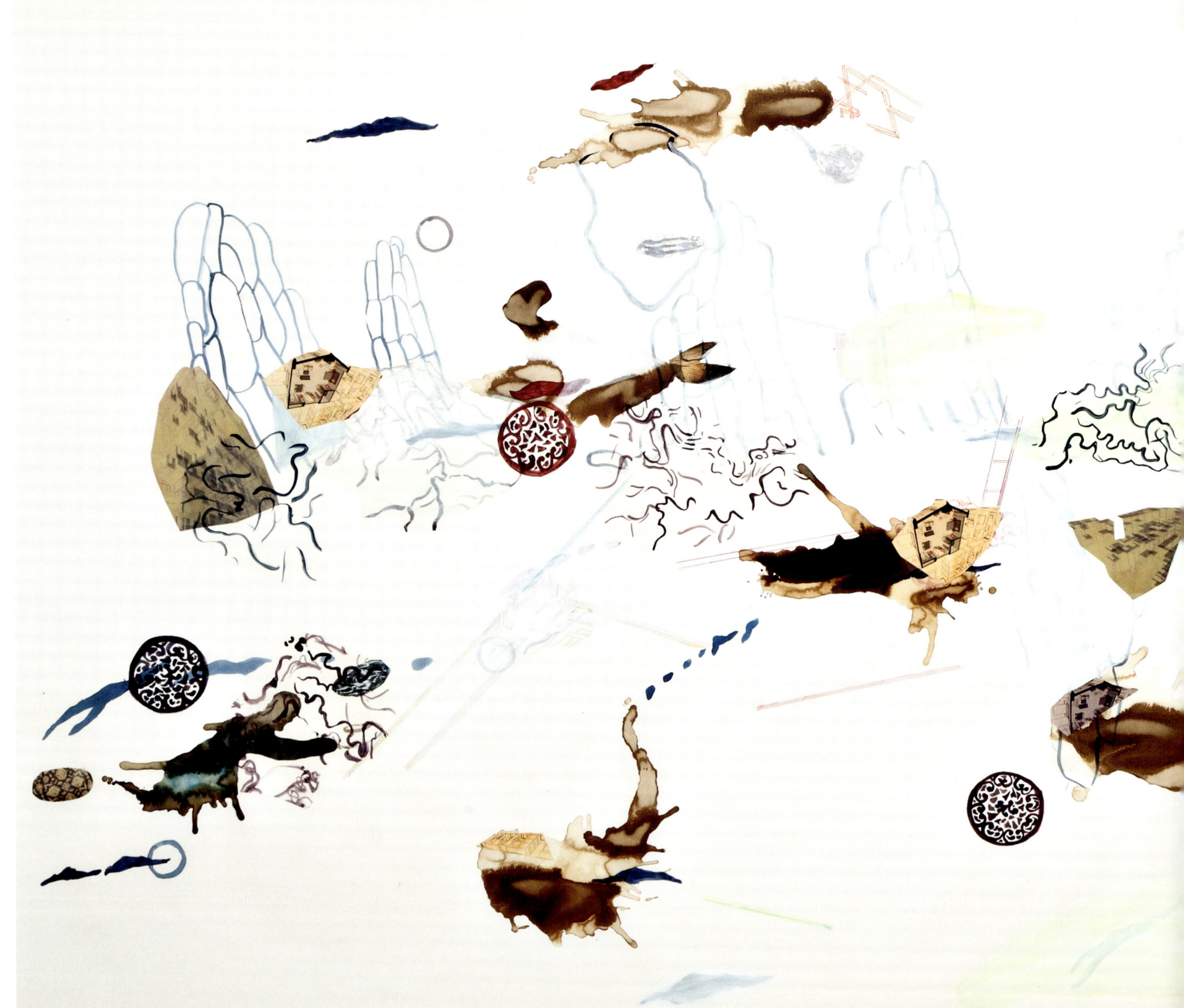

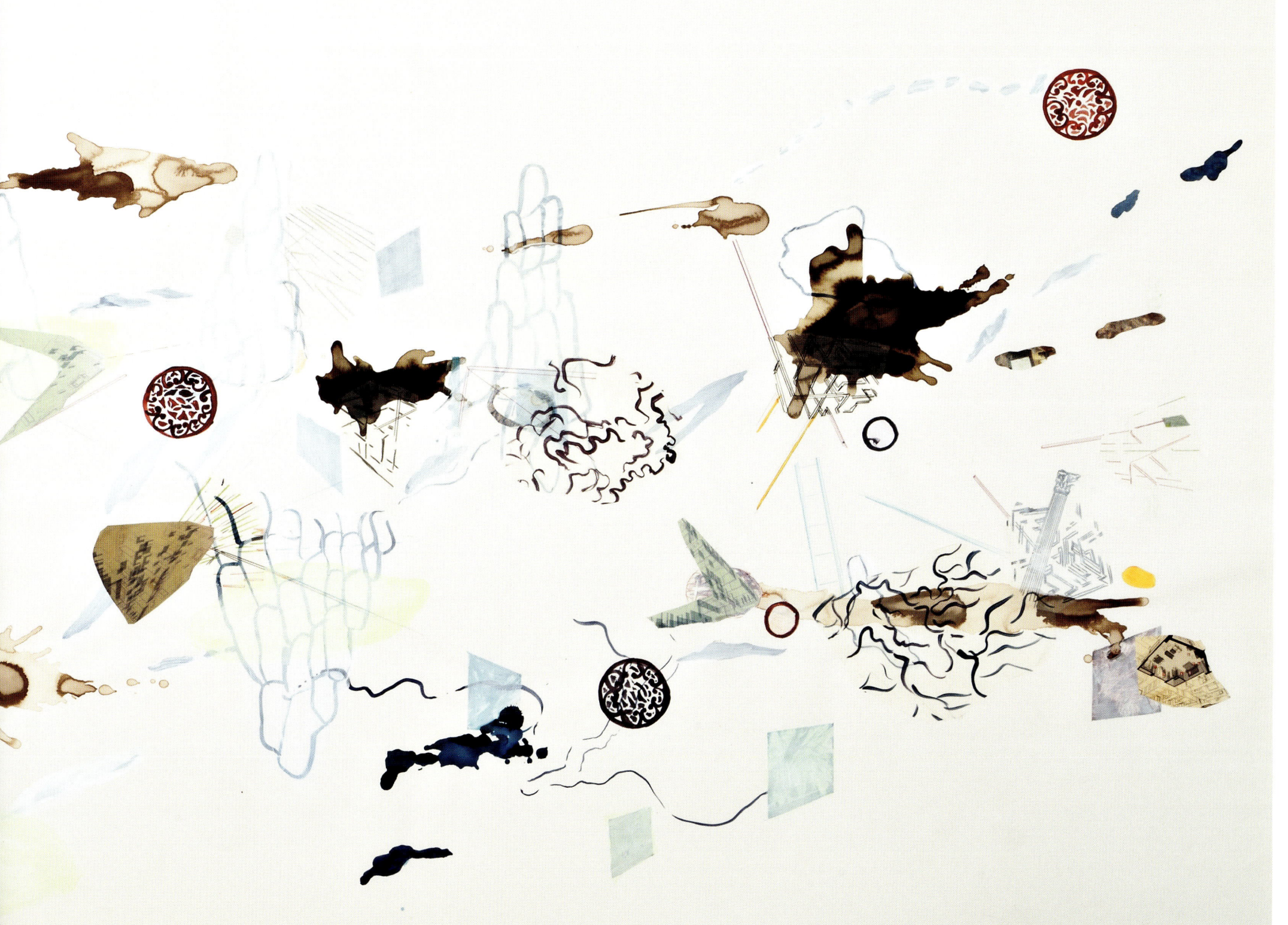

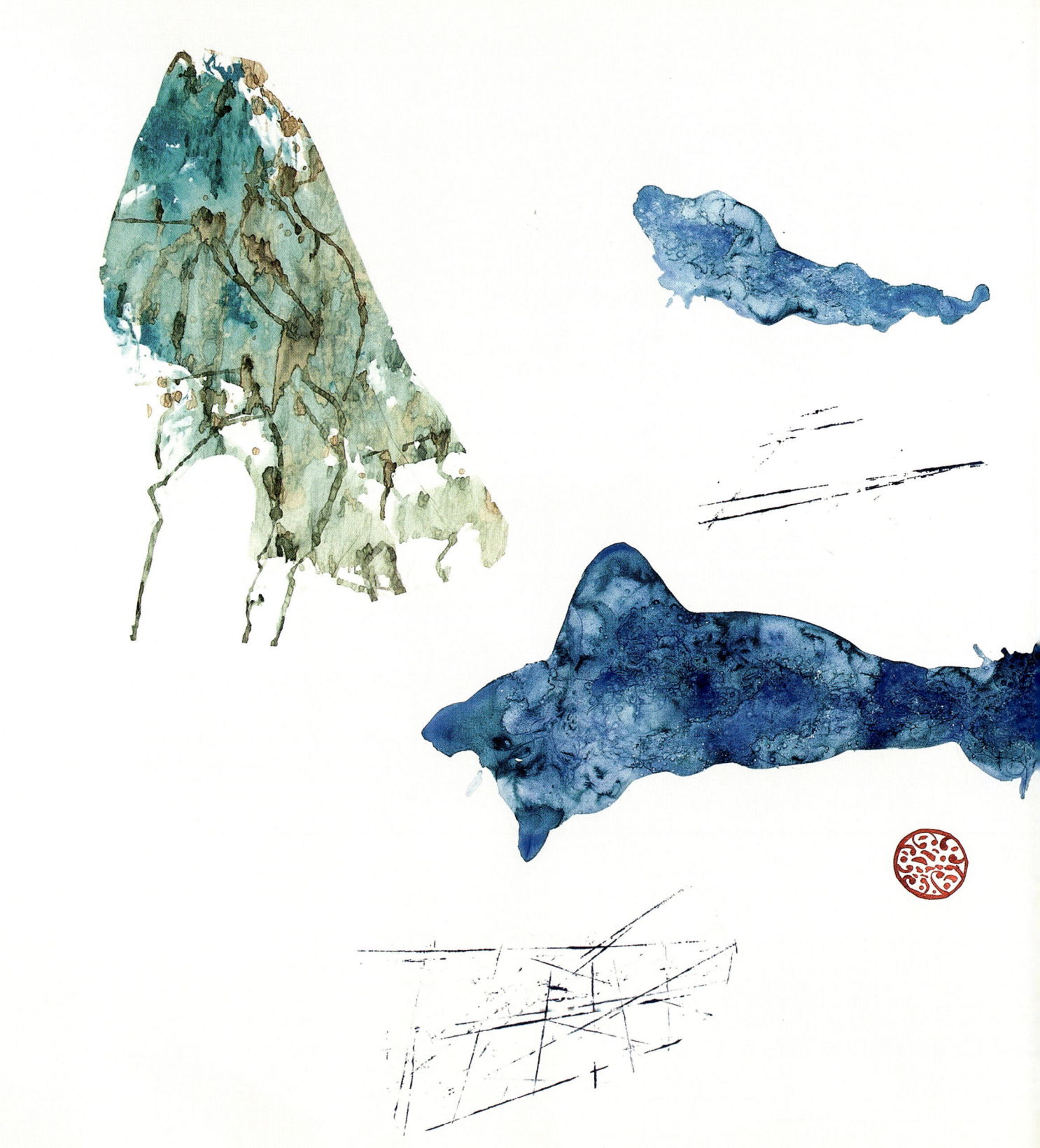

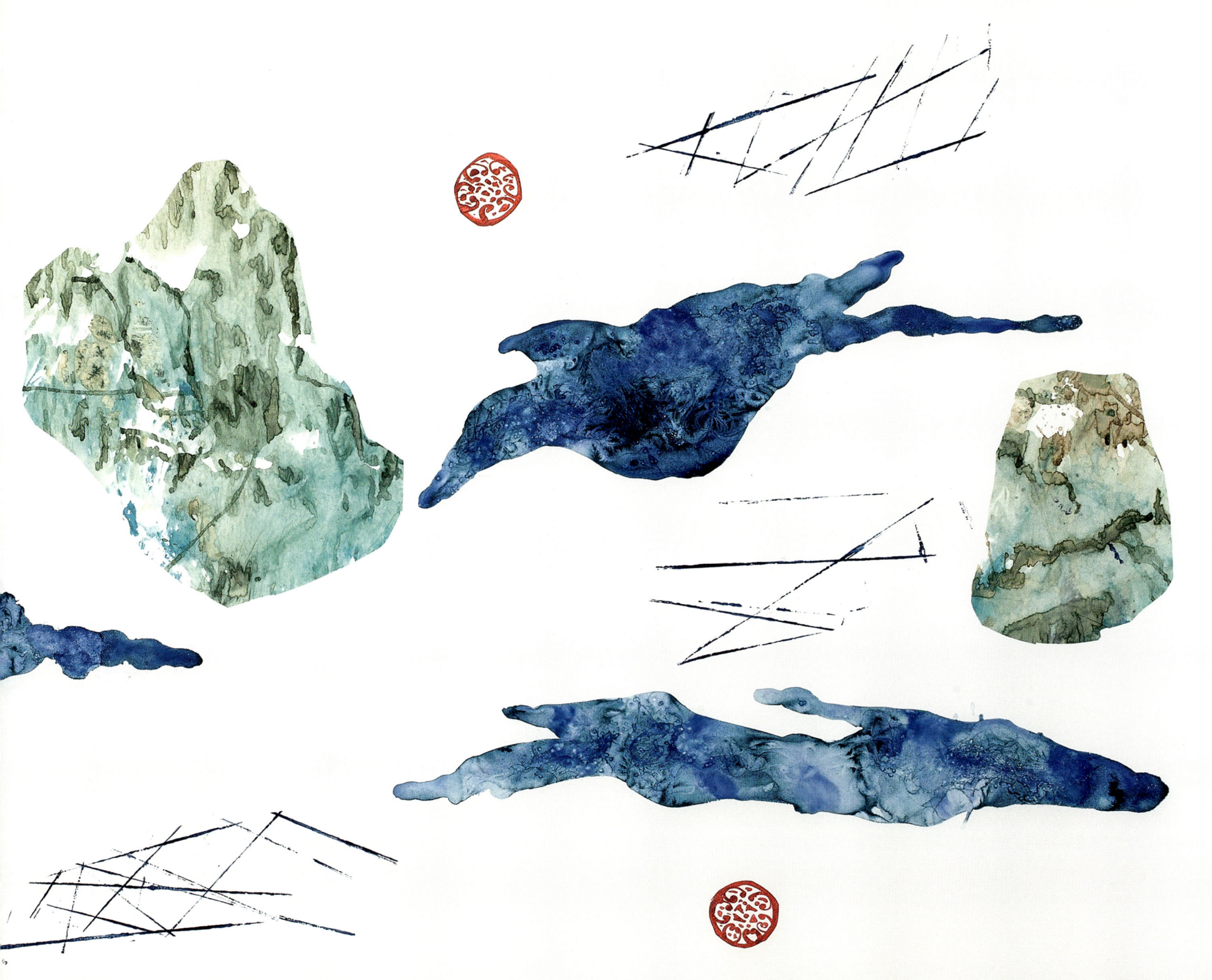

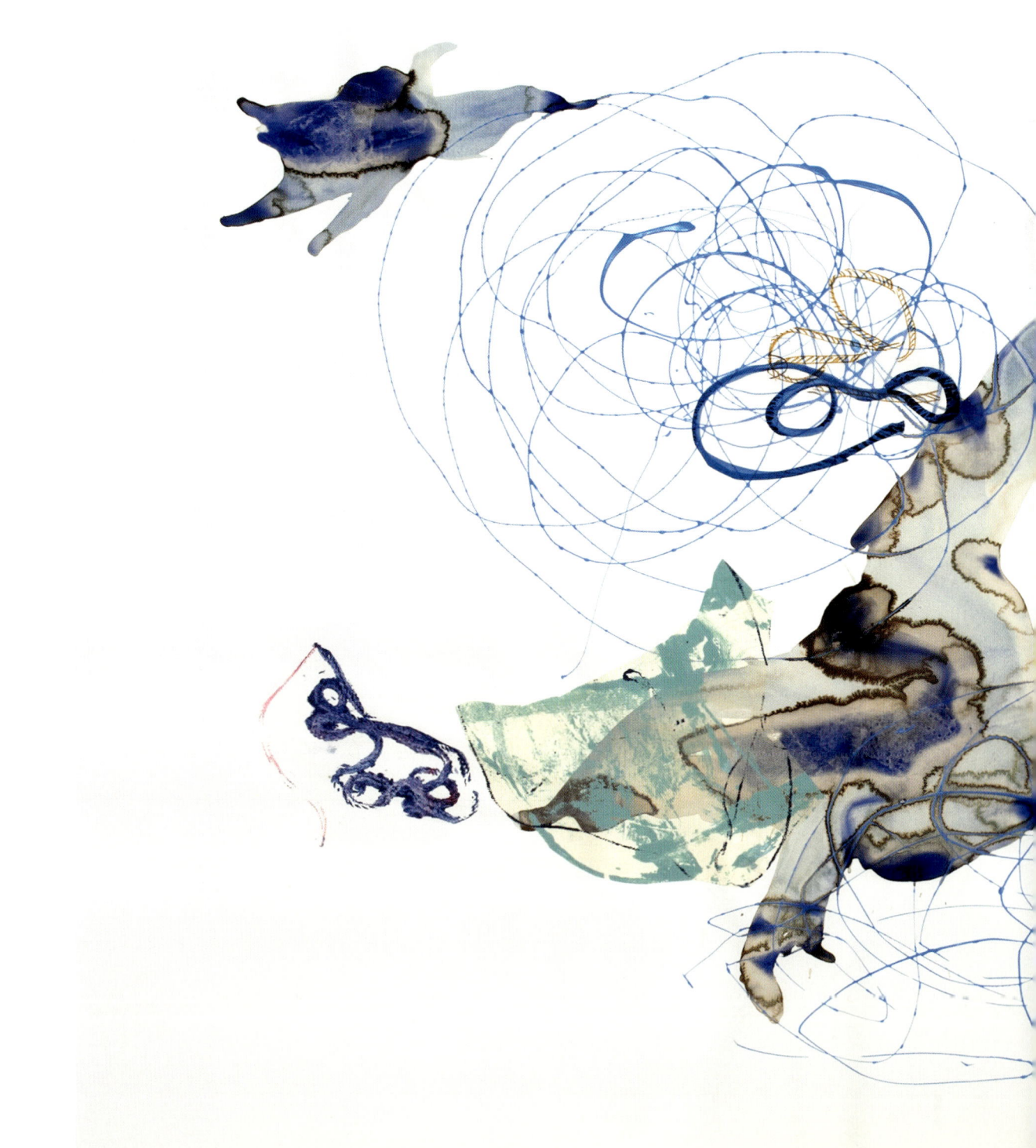

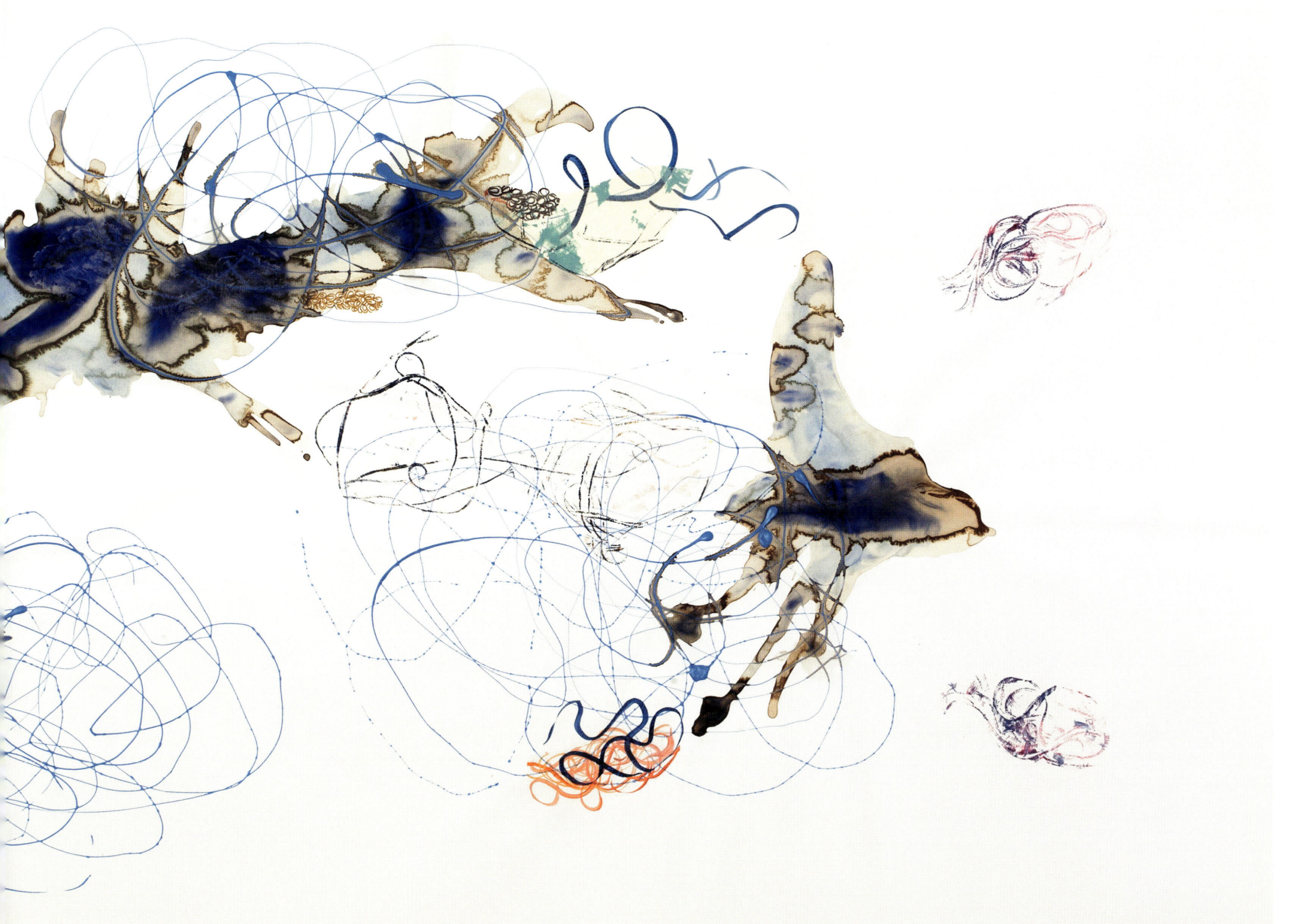

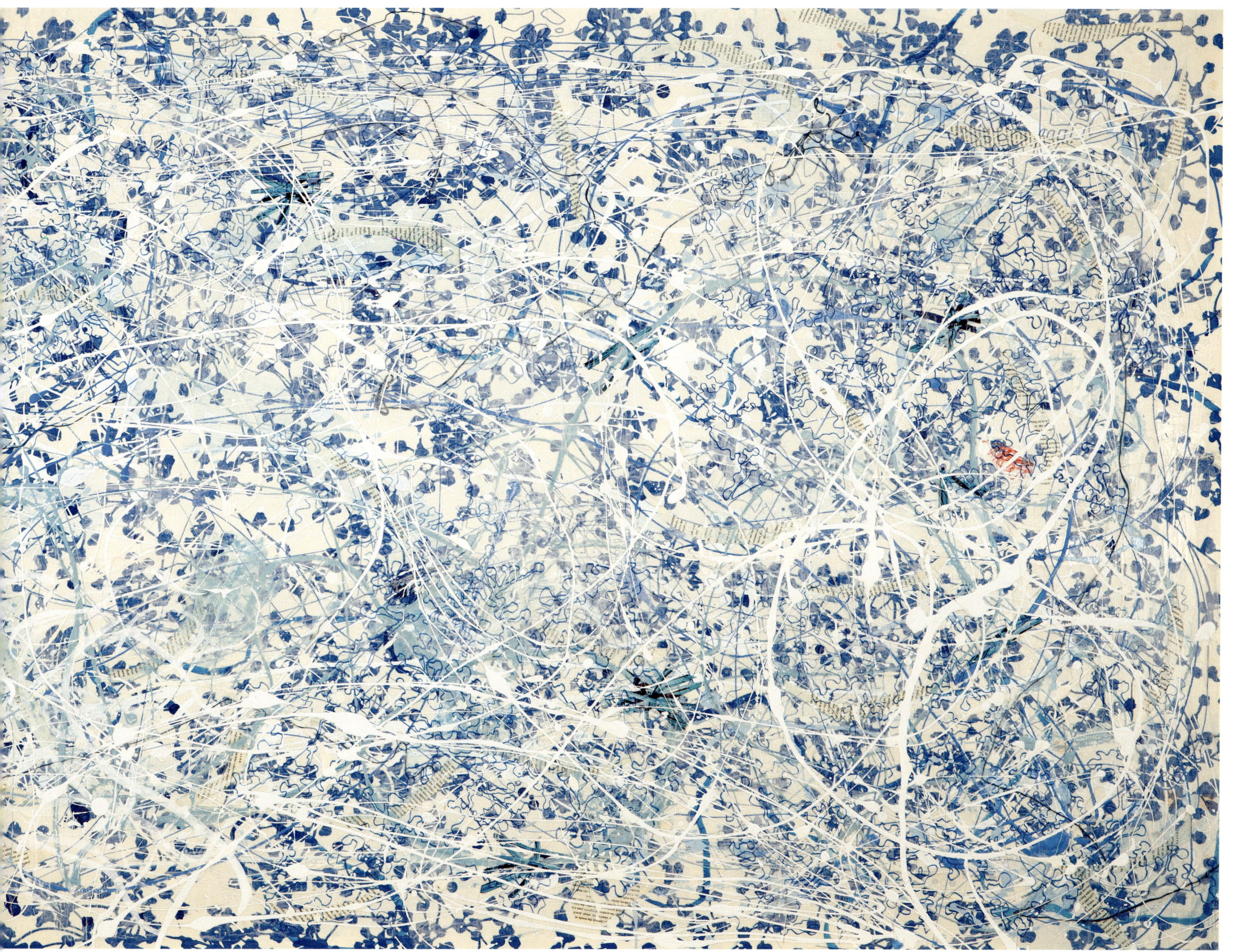

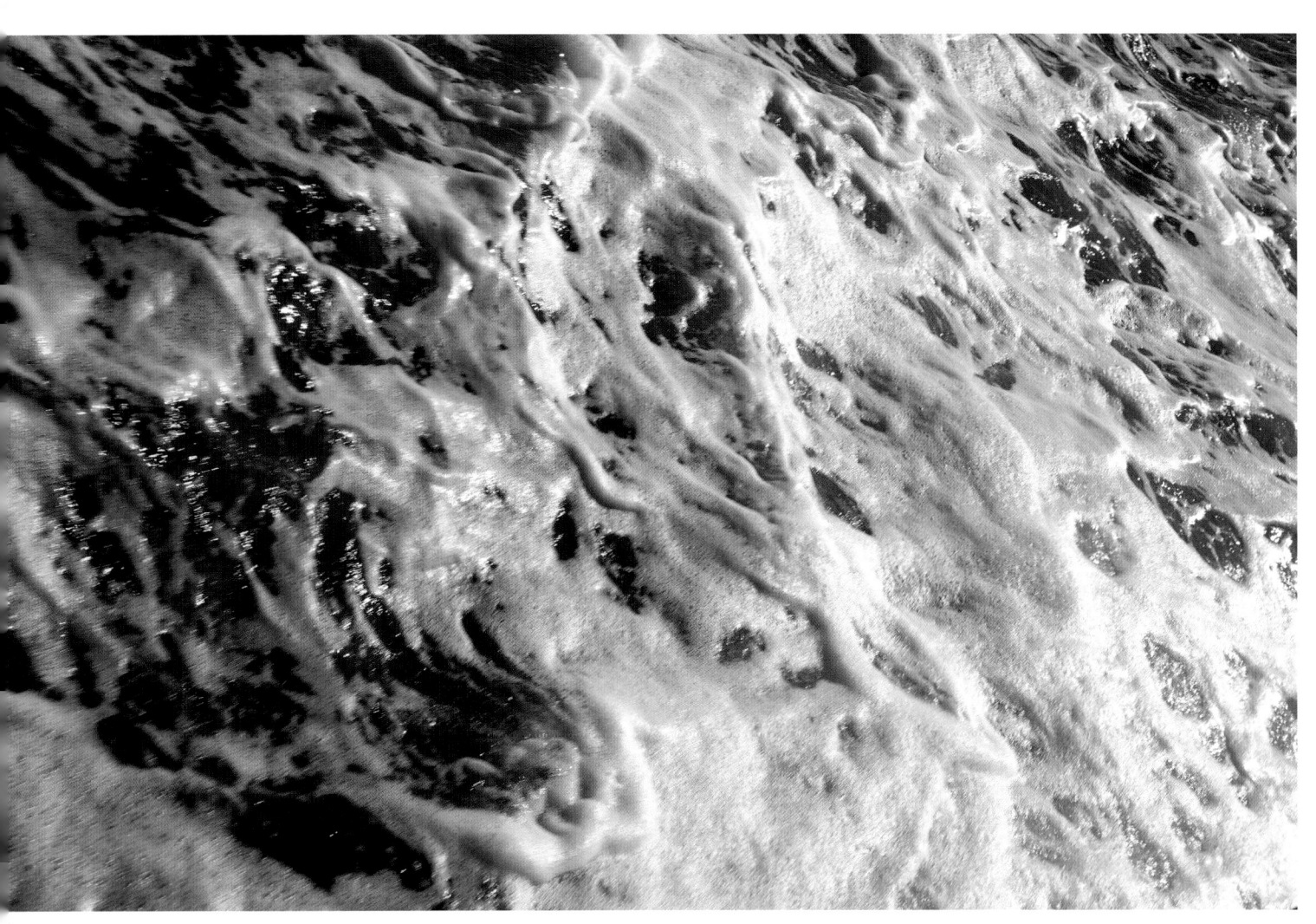

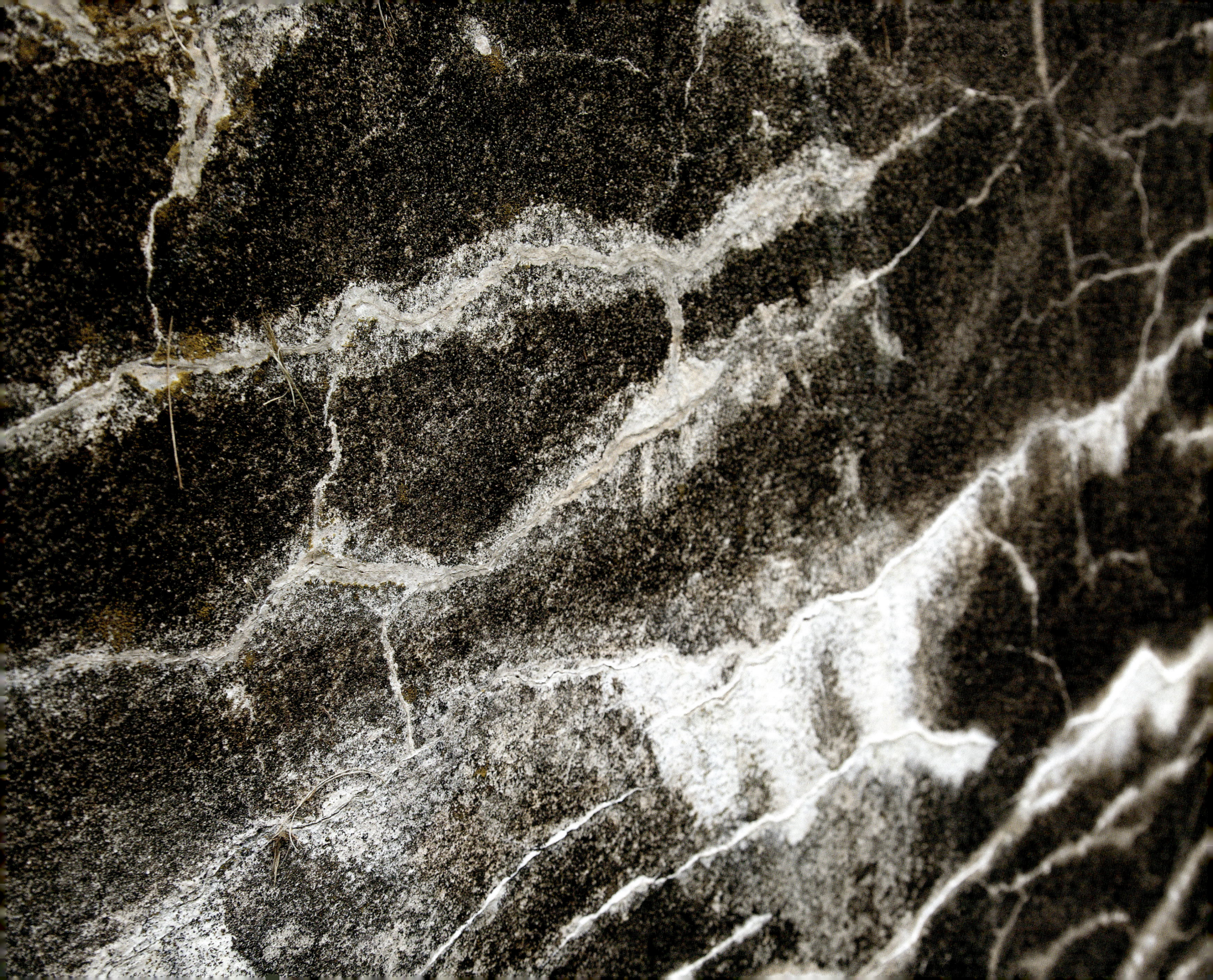

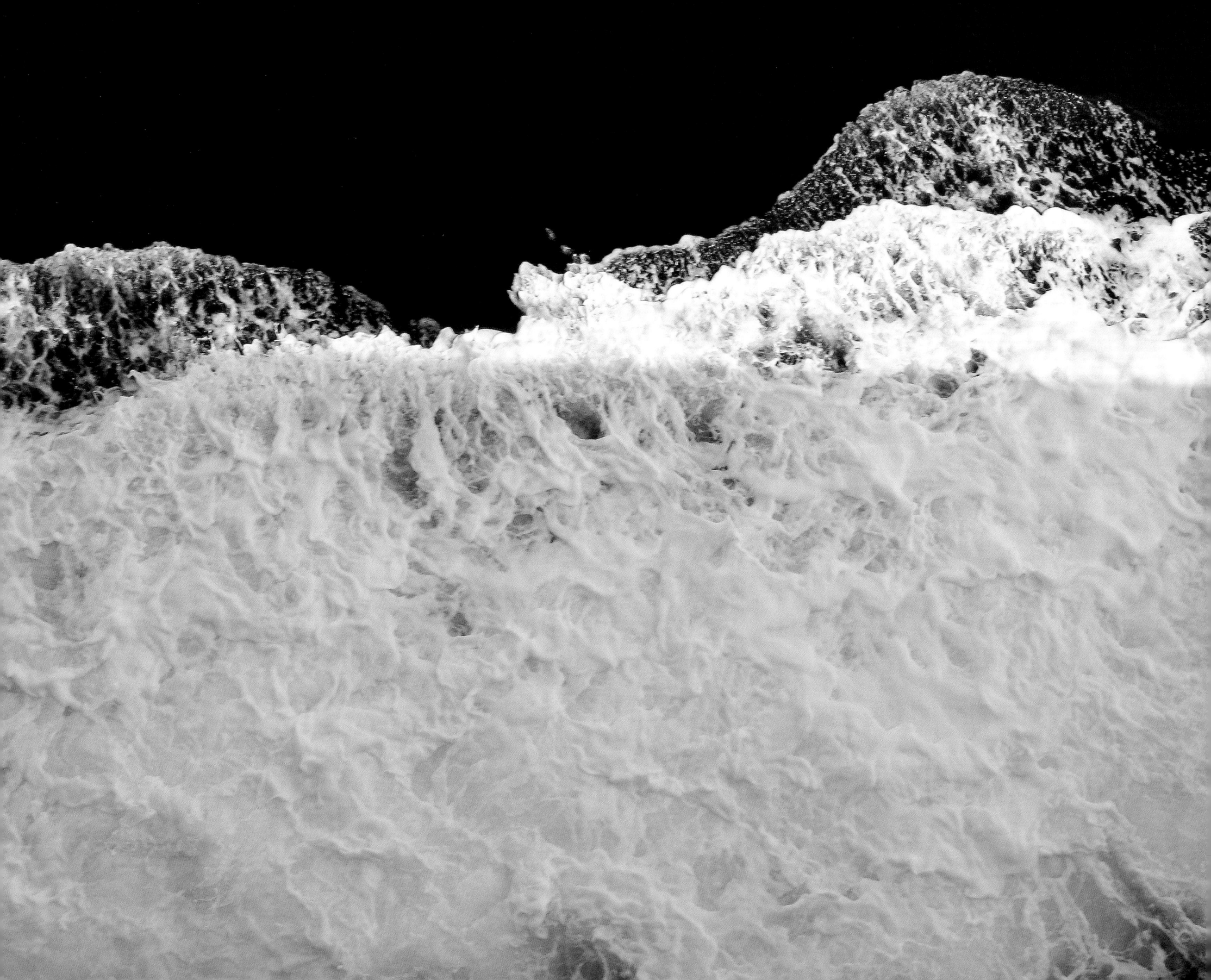

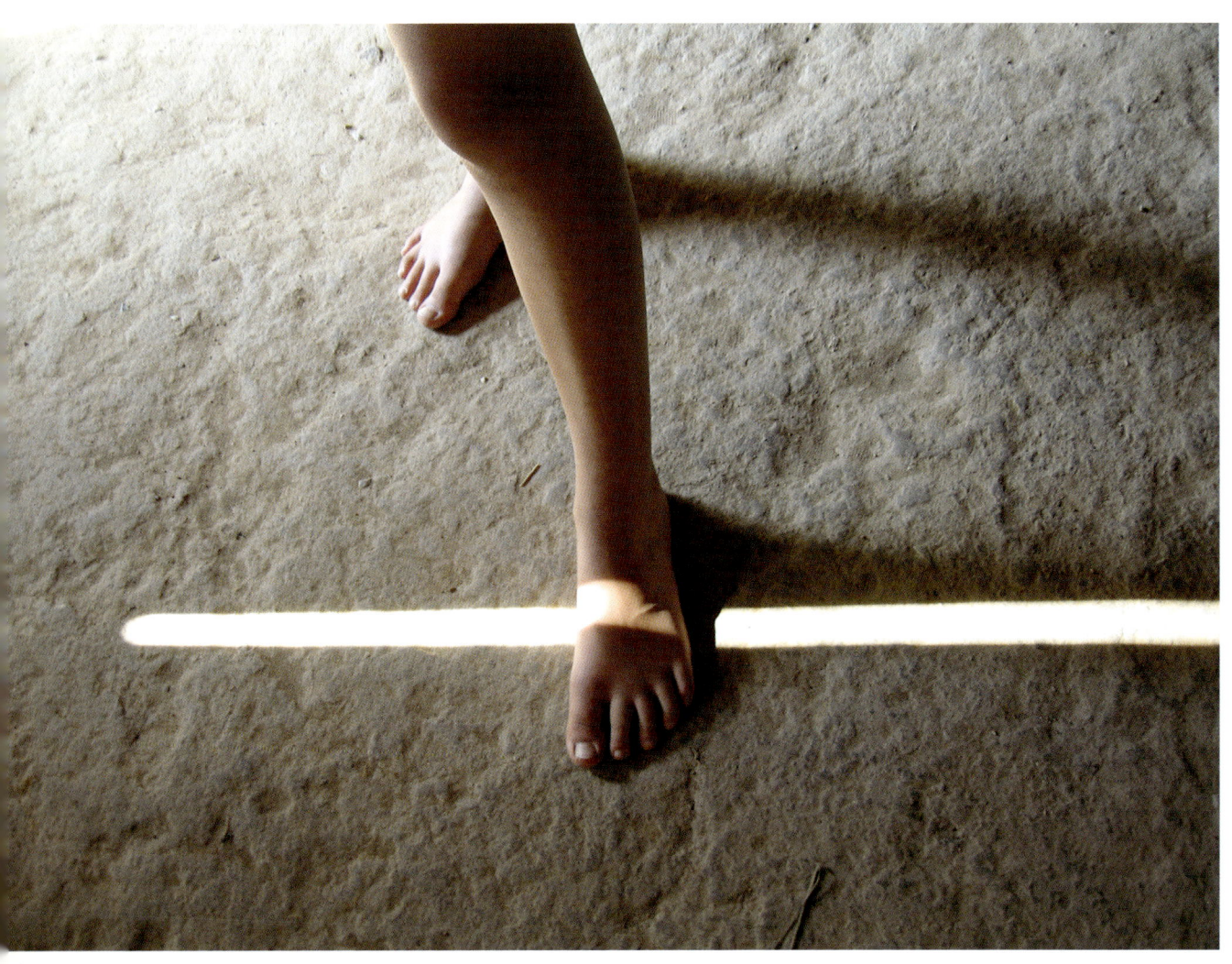

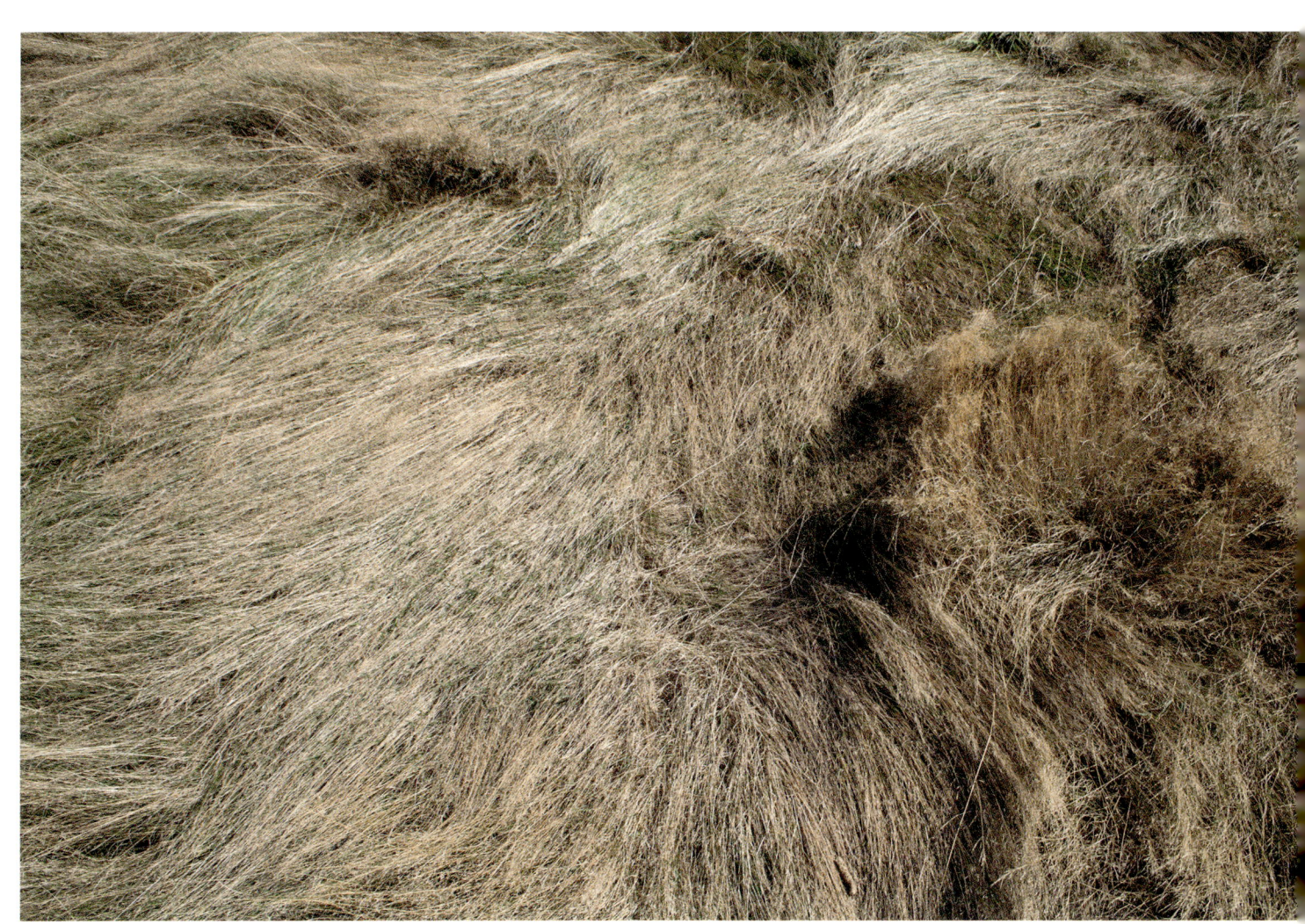

Thanks

Many thanks to the team at jovis: Jochen Visscher for collaborating on yet another exciting book project, Susanne Rösler for her always inspiring design contributions, Philipp Sperrle for his organizational input, and Jutta Bornholdt-Cassetti for her great PR work.

I would like to give my profound gratitude to Nessia Pope for her thoughtful interview and for being willing to engage herself with the different layers of my artistic process. I also thank Edwina van Gal for going over the interview with open eyes, and Paulina Pardo.

Many thanks to Frank Maresca, Roger Ricco, and Elenore Weber of the Ricco/Maresca Gallery for believing in my work and showing it so beautifully.

I wish to thank Kevin Miller and the Southeast Museum of Photography for being so supportive and exhibiting *Home Stills* in great depth. The same is true for the Houston Center for Photography, especially Bevin Berin Dubrovski and Libbie Masterson.

Thanks to Adrienne Conzelman and her gallery ARC Fine Art and Jayne Baum from the JHB Gallery for showcasing my different projects over the years so professionally; Thanks go also to Glynis Berry from Art Sites for showing Topos, as well as to Harper Levine for showing *Home Stills* at Harper's. I wish to thank Chris Vroom and Catherine Levene from Artspace for presenting my art so skillfully in the digital world; and Edward Gomez for our interesting cross-cultural art dialogue.

Many thanks to Toni Ross for your friendship and sisterhood, for sharing adventures and inspiring me, for exploring different artistic and cultural turfs together—whether in Egypt, Paris, Burma or right at home.

Thanks to Liz and Kirk Radke, for your friendship, your loyalty, and continued artistic support; Huberta von Voss and Peter Wittig for your friendship and your incredible energy in bringing people together meaningfully; to Ed Osowski for being a long-time friend and supporter of my projects; to Anita Naughton for your insights, laughter, and years of friendship. And thanks to Carolin Bohlmann, Alessandra Brunialti, Nanao Anton, Ron Kaplan, Janice Stanton, Bernadette Gotthardt, and Hans-Georg Pospischil for your friendship and artistic support.

A big thanks to Charline Spector from Bookhampton for your deep insights about life and family, and for your belief that books make the world a better place, and for being such a supporter of *Home Stills*.

Thanks to all of the community out East; it's one of the greatest places to live and work.

And thanks to my mother Uta, for fostering an atmosphere of creativity and freedom and for letting us wander; and to my siblings Pascale, Florian, Benjamin, Sophie and their families. Growing up together in Greece was a life-altering and meaningful adventure.

I love you Max, Julian, and Philippe! What a beautiful journey of life we have shared, I could not have done it without you! Thanks for accompanying me on the adventurous forays into known and unknown countries. It's always great to travel together, whether to Japan, Greece, or Germany.

This book is dedicated to all the wanderers—either on foot or in their minds—the daydreamers, the quiet ones, this one is for you.

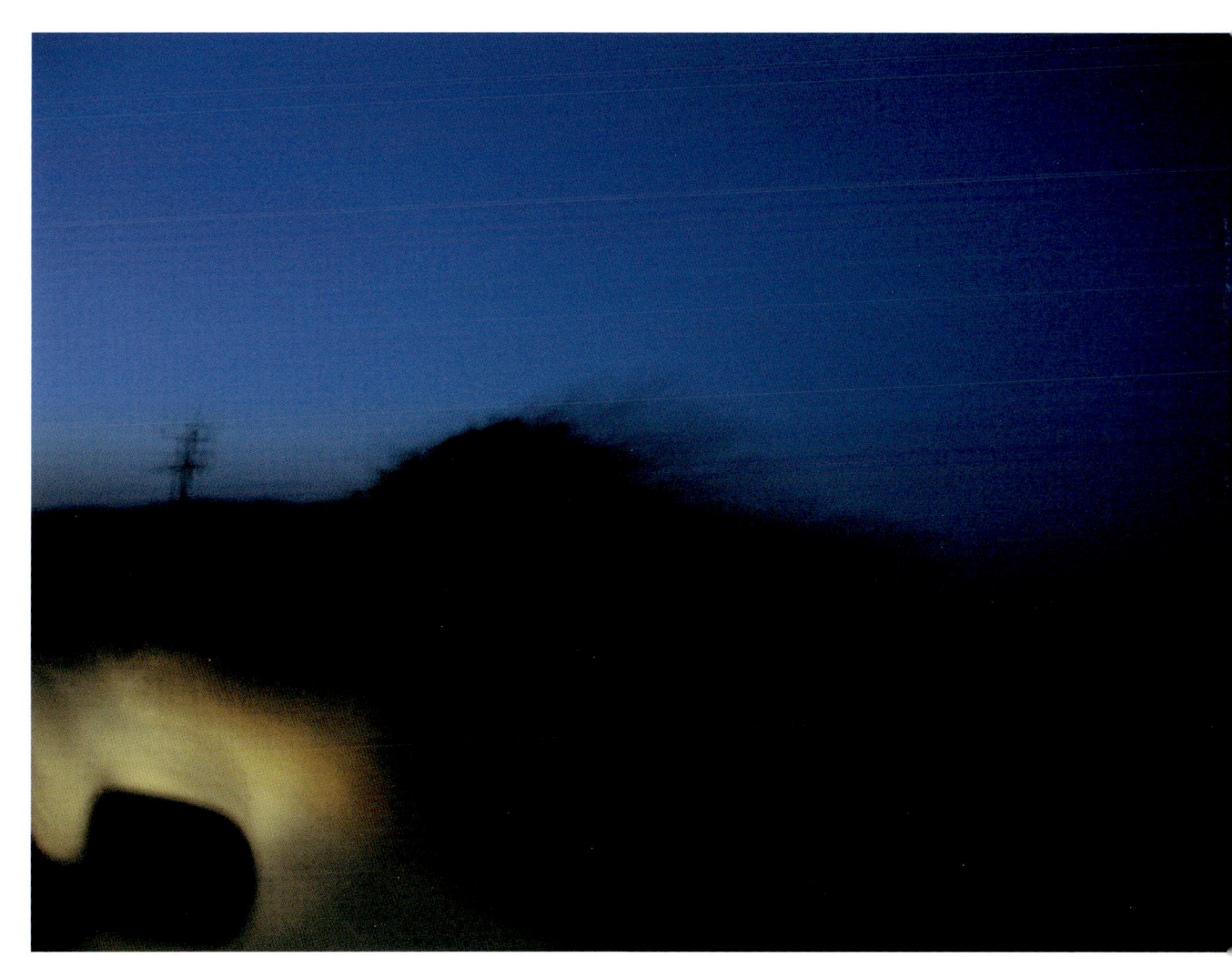

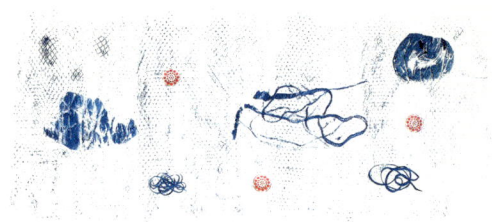

Untitled
2012
Mixed media on paper, 42 × 88 inches

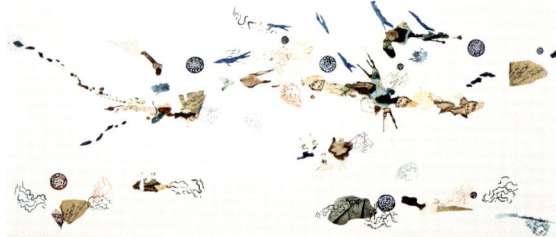

Untitled
2010
Mixed media on paper, 42 × 95 inches

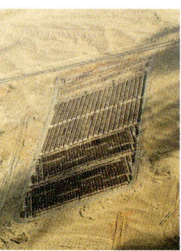

Desert buildings, Cairo, Egypt
2010

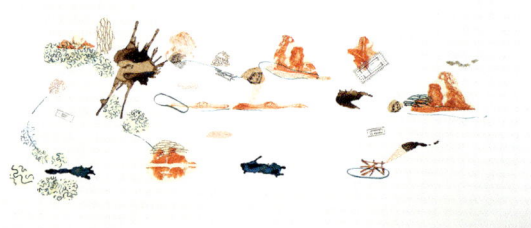

Untitled
2011
Mixed media on paper, 42 × 92 inches

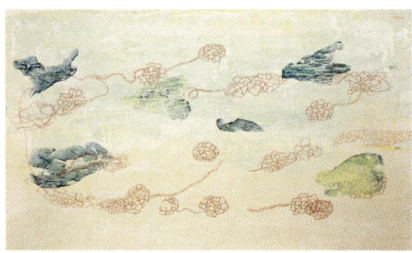

Untitled
2010
Mixed media on paper, 41 × 69 inches

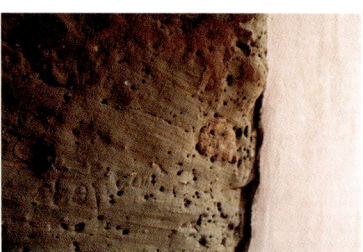

Cave, Bagan, Burma
2012

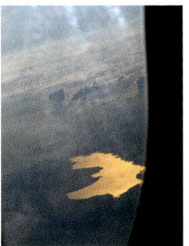

Golden lake, Greece
2011

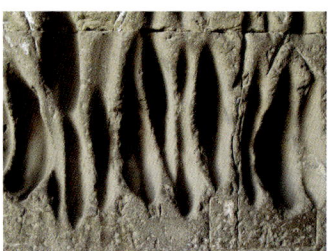

Markings, Edfu Temple, Luxor, Egypt
2010

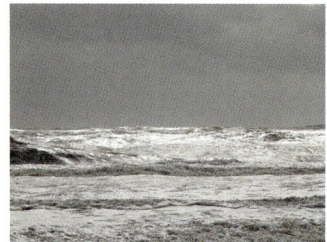

Ocean, Bridgehampton
2012

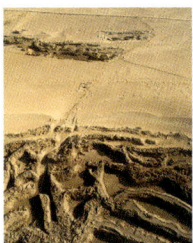

Desert, Egypt
2010

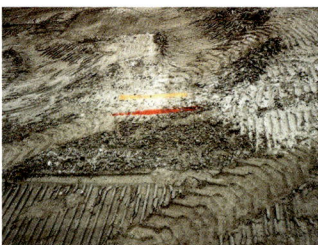

Construction site, Palm Beach, Florida
2006

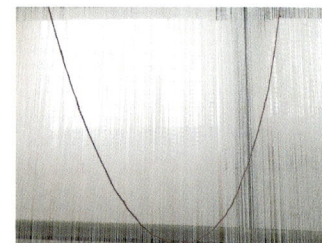

Carpet strings, Sakkara, Egypt
2010

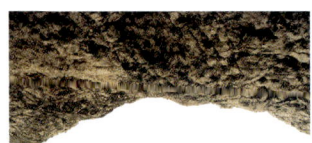

Cave, Balos, Greece
2012

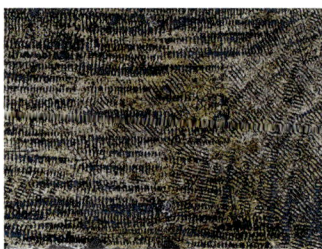

Ibn Tulum Mosque, Cairo, Egypt
2010

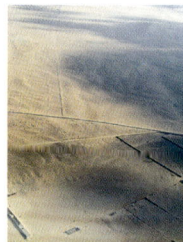

Desert paths, Cairo, Egypt
2010

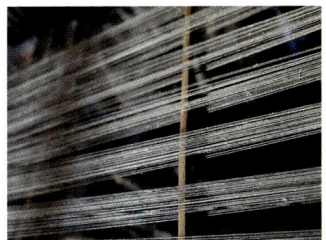

Loom, Mrauk U, Burma
2012

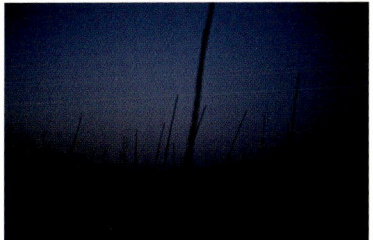

Stakes, Inle lake, Burma
2012

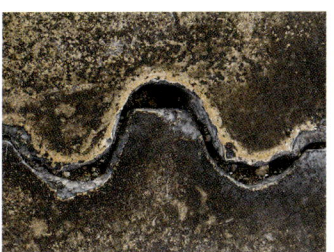

Mosque of Ibn Tulum, Cairo, Egypt
2010

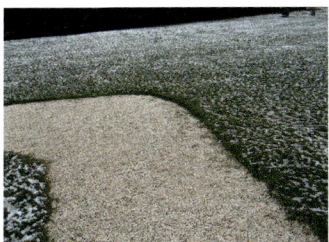

Path, Bridgehampton
2009

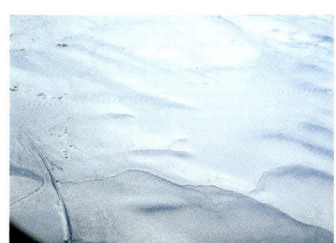

Patagonia
2005

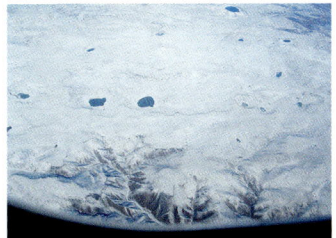

Patagonia
2005

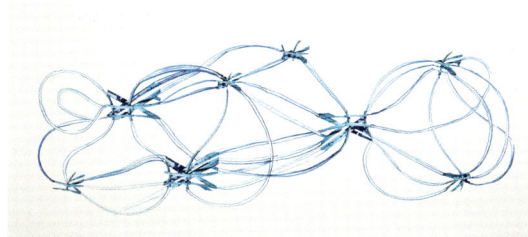

Untitled
2010
Mixed media on paper, 36 × 88 inches

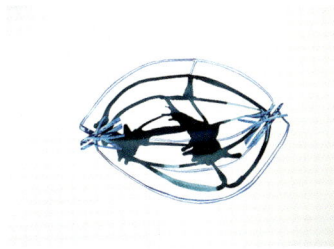

Untitled
2010
Mixed media on paper, 22 × 30 inches

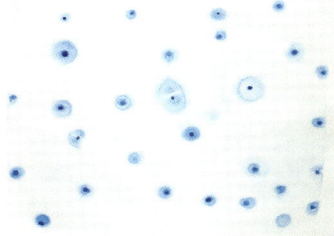

Untitled
2010
Mixed media on paper, 22 × 30 inches

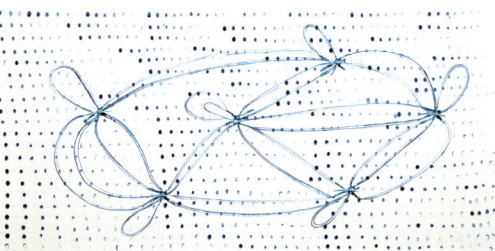

Untitled
2010
Mixed media on paper, 36 × 75 inches

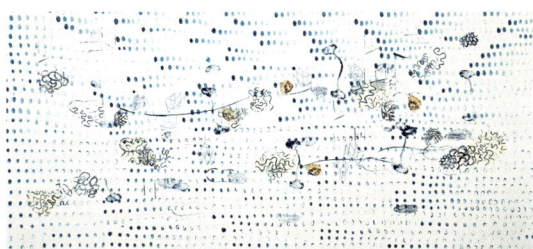

Untitled
2010
Mixed media on paper, 42 × 88 inches

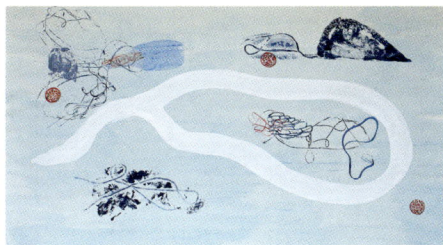

Untitled
2010
Mixed media on paper, 36 × 65 inches

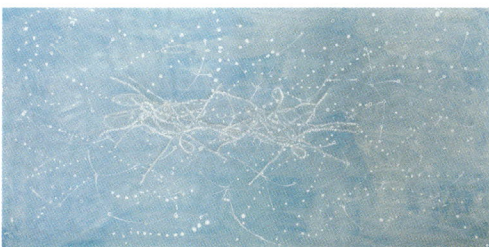

Untitled
2012
Mixed media on paper, 36 × 70 inches

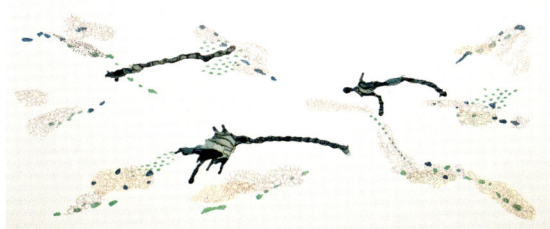

Untitled
2010
Mixed media on paper, 36 × 78 inches

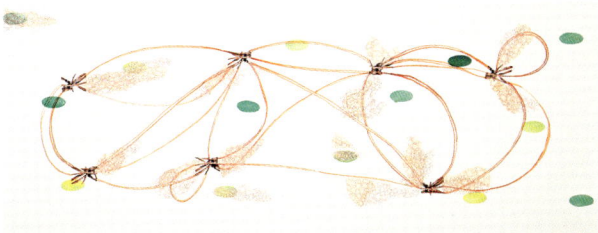

Untitled
2010
Mixed media on paper, 36 × 85 inches

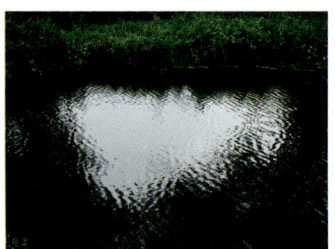

River, Lenzen, Germany
2007

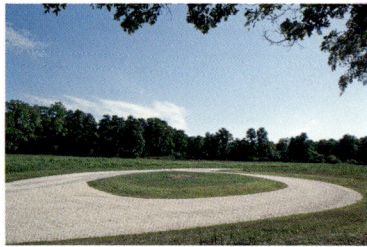

Driveway, Shelter Island
2009

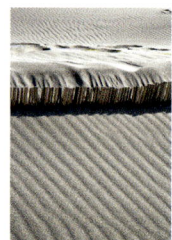

Beach, Hamamatsu, Japan,
2007

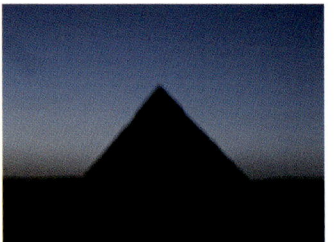

Pyramid, Cairo, Egypt
2010

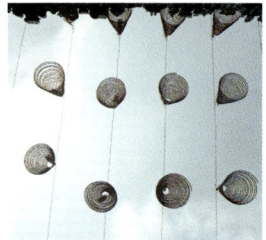

Incense, Ho Chi Minh City, Vietnam
2006

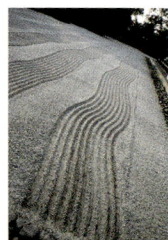

Imperial Garden, Kyoto, Japan
2007

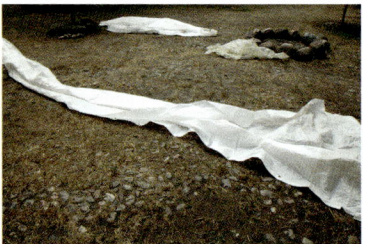

Tarps, Strehlen, Germany
2007

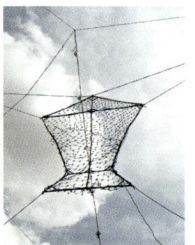

Lights, Cairo, Egypt
2010

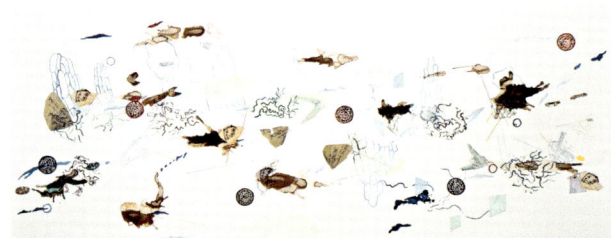

Untitled
2010
Mixed media on paper, 42 x 102 inches

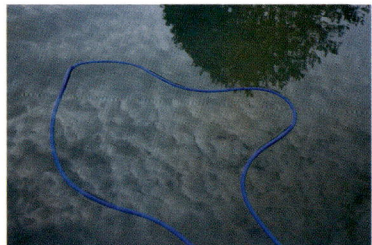

Hose, Shelter Island
2011

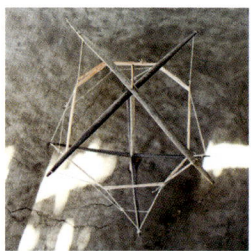

Spindle, Mrauk U, Burma
2012

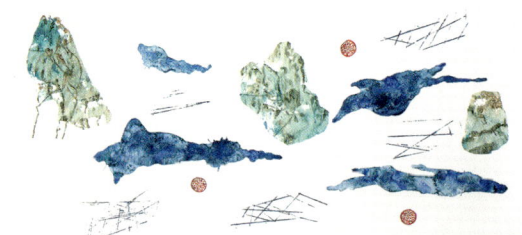

Untitled
2013
Mixed media on paper, 42 x 90 inches

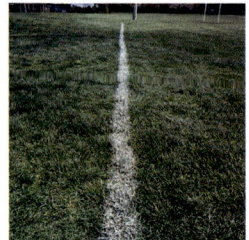

Sports field, Easthampton
2006

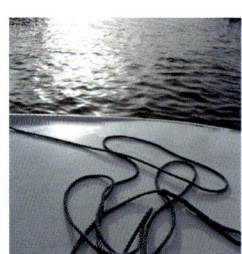

Ropes, Luxor, Egypt
2010

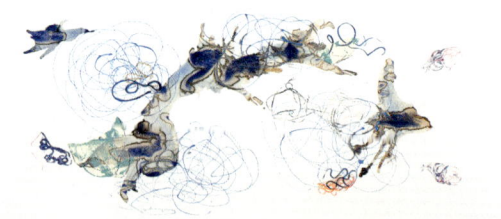

Untitled
2011
Mixed media on paper, 42 x 88 inches

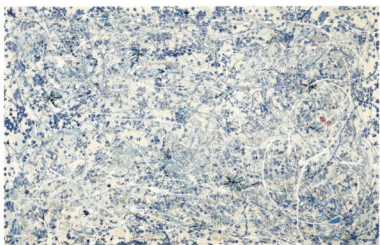

Untitled
2010
Mixed media on canvas, 48 × 72 inches

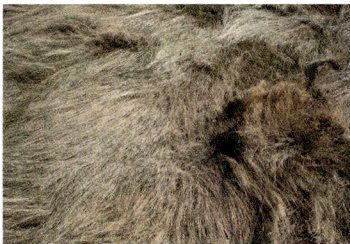

Underbrush, Shelter Island
2008

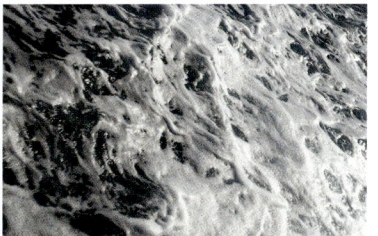

Waves, Samos, Greece
2012

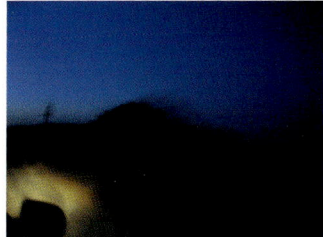

Car ride, Samos, Greece
2005

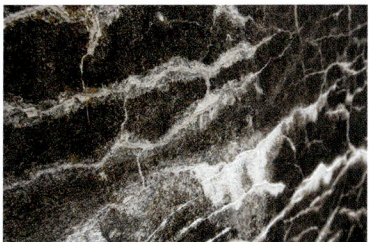

Wall, Shelter Island
2009

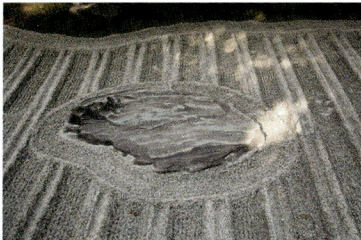

Garden, Kyoto, Japan
2007

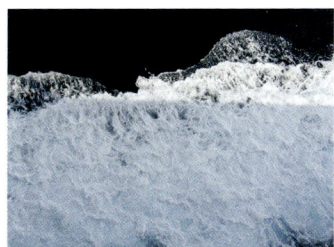

Water, Samos
2005

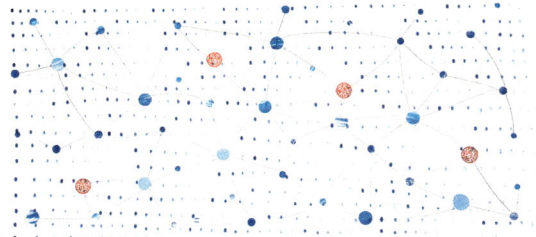

Untitled
2012
Mixed media on paper, 42 × 90 inches

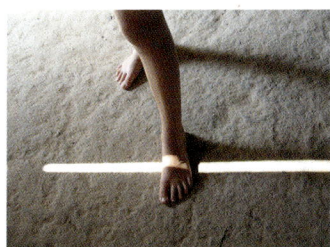

Measuring light, Strehlen, Germany
2008

Bastienne Schmidt

is a mixed media artist living in Bridgehampton and New York. She also has lived and worked for many years in Greece, Italy, and Germnay.

Her photographic work is included in the collections of the Museum of Modern Art in New York, the International Center of Photography, The Brooklyn Museum, The Victoria and Albert Museum in London, the Bibliotheque Nationale in Paris among many others. Her work has been widely exhibited nationally and internationally.
She has previously published *Vivir la Muerte*, *American Dreams*, *Shadow Home* and *Home Stills*.
Topography of Quiet will be her fifth book.

Nessia Pope

Nessia Pope is a Brazilian Curator and journalist living in New York.

She has worked with many museums, institutions and galleries in New York and Brazil for the past 20 years, such as the Museum of Modern Art in Rio de Janeiro and the Museum of Modern Art in São Paulo. She has written a book *Contemporary Art in Manhattan* and has been curator at Artspace.com since its inception.

Public Collections

Bibliotheque Nationale, Paris, France
Brooklyn Museum, Brooklyn, NY
Center for Creative Photography, Tucson, AZ
Corcoran Gallery of Art, Washington, DC
Guild Hall, East Hampton, NY
International Center for Photography, New York, NY
Museum of Fine Arts, Houston, TX
The Museum of Modern Art, New York, NY
Museum für Kunst und Gewerbe, Hamburg, Germany
Museet Fotografiska, Stockholm, Schweden
Norton Museum of Art, West Palm Beach, FL
Southeast Museum of Photography, Florida
Worcester Art Museum, Worcester, MA
University of Texas, San Antonio, TX
Victoria and Albert Museum, London, England

www.bastienneschmidt.com

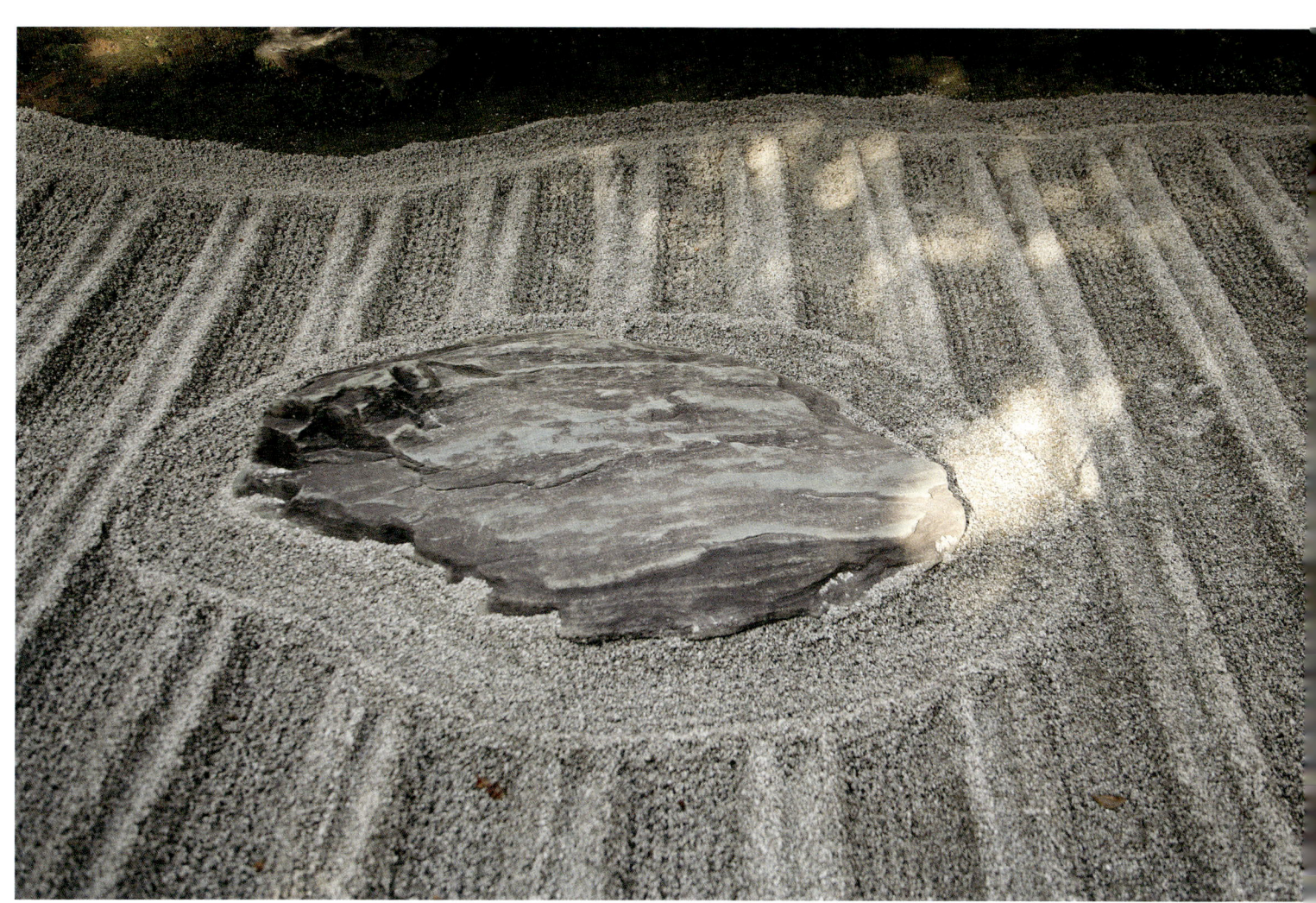

© 2013 by jovis Verlag GmbH
Texts by kind permission of the authors.
Pictures by kind permission of Bastienne Schmidt.

Concept: Bastienne Schmidt
Design: Bastienne Schmidt, Susanne Rösler
Lithography: Bild I Druck, Berlin
Printing and binding: GCC Grafisches Centrum Cuno

Bibliographic information published by the Deutsche Nationalbibliothek
The Deutsche Nationalbibliothek lists this publication in the Deutsche
Nationalbibliografie; detailed bibliographic data are available on the
Internet at http://dnb.d-nb.de

jovis books are available worldwide in selected bookstores. Please contact
your nearest bookseller or visit www.jovis.de for information concerning
your local distribution.

jovis Verlag GmbH
Kurfürstenstraße 15/16
10785 Berlin

www.jovis.de

ISBN 978-3-86859-260-3

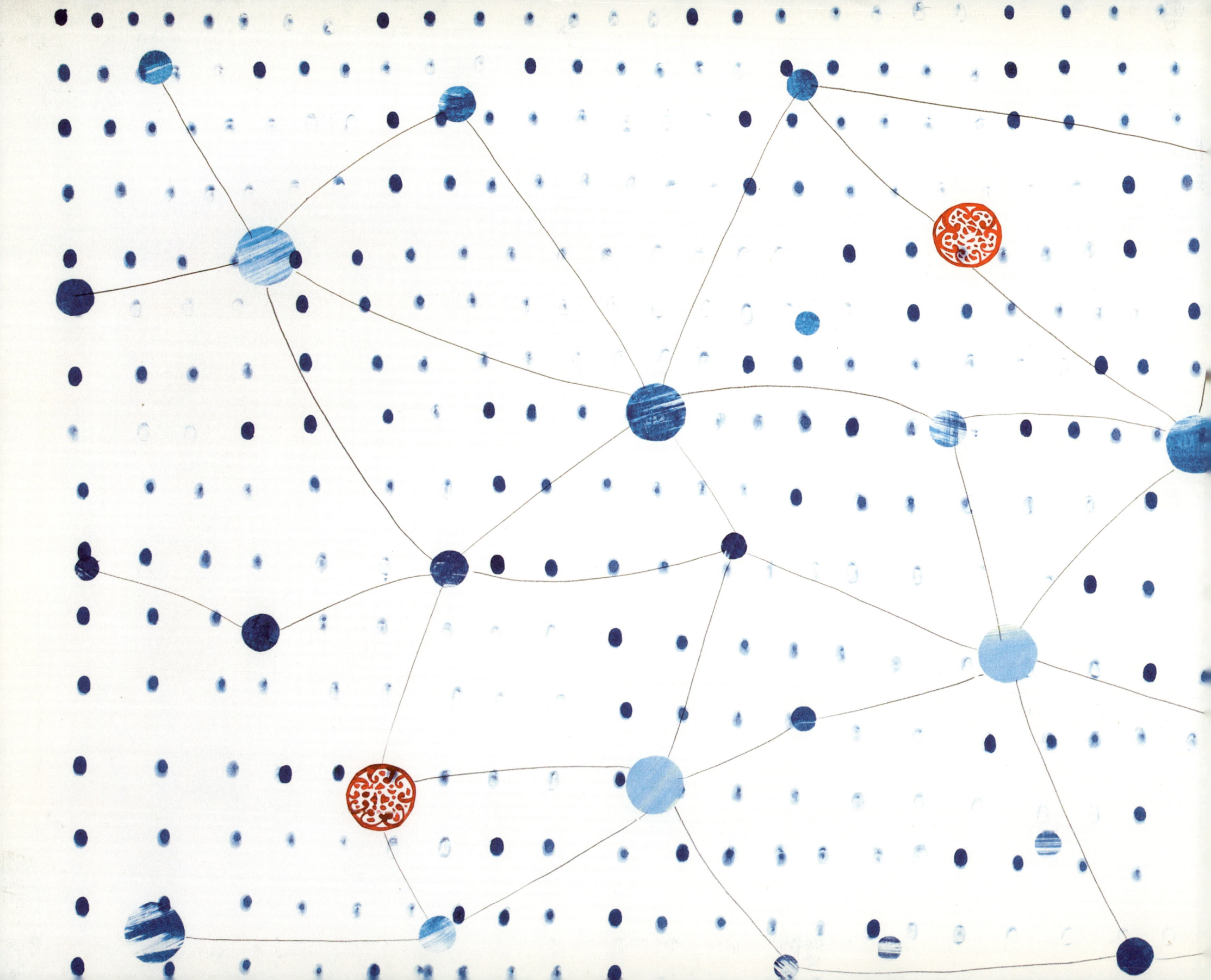